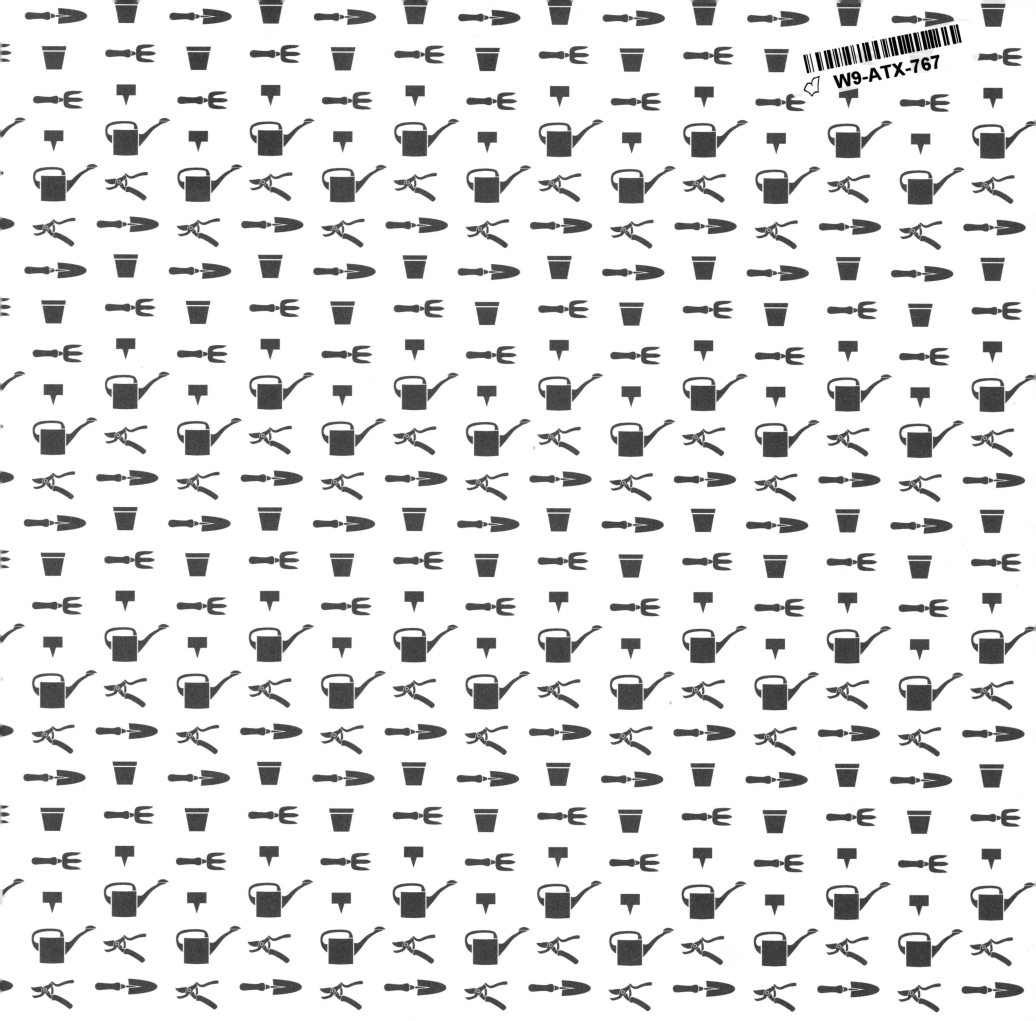

Start to plant
GARDENS & CONTAINERS

Create your ideal garden with these simple-to-follow projects

Graham A. Pavey

CHARTWELL
BOOKS, INC.

A QUINTET BOOK

Published by Chartwell Books
A Division of Book Sales, Inc.
114 Northfield Avenue
Edison, New Jersey 08837

This edition produced for sale in the U.S.A., its
territories and dependencies only.

ISBN 0-7858-0595-8

This book was designed and produced by
Quintet Publishing Limited
6 Blundell Street
London N7 9BH

Creative Director: Richard Dewing
Designer: James Lawrence
Project Editor: Diana Steedman
Editor: Janet Swarbrick
Photographer: Keith Waterton

Typeset in Great Britain by
Central Southern Typesetters, Eastbourne
Manufactured by Bright Arts (Singapore) Pte Ltd
Printed by Leefung-Asco Printers Ltd, China

CONTENTS

HERB GARDENS
...97

ROCK & ALPINE GARDENS
...145

CONTAINER GARDENS

*Easy-to-follow projects
to create impressive container plantings
to enhance your whole garden*

INTRODUCTION

N o garden is complete without carefully placed ornaments and planted containers, and where space is limited, such as on a balcony or in a tiny backyard, containers may form the complete garden. Professionally planted flowers, herbs, fruit, and vegetables overflowing from pots and tubs, cascading from hanging baskets and swelling window boxes look stunning – but can they be achieved by the layman? The answer is YES, as long as some simple rules are followed and a sound aftercare regime is pursued.

This book will show how, with a little know-how, some forethought, and care, it is possible to create impressive container plantings that will enhance the whole garden. The secret is in the preparation, choice of plants, attention to feeding, watering, and caring for your new garden feature.

Most smaller containers are mobile and can easily be moved to anywhere in the garden, but it is important to position large permanent containers in the right place. Their positioning in the garden can be critical – for instance, a well-placed empty flowerpot can look more attractive than an award-winning container of moisture- and shade-loving plants that have dried up in drought conditions in full sun.

We explore the best ways to use containers in the garden, the different types of containers, and the tools, materials, and techniques required for planting them up and aftercare of your plants. Nineteen easy-to-follow projects are described with clear instructions on how to get the best from your container plants.

MATERIALS AND TECHNIQUES

Containers are available in a wide range of shapes, sizes, and materials.

Containers

Terra-cotta is probably the best choice of material for pots and containers. It is kind to plants, retaining moisture and keeping the roots cool, and looks good in most garden styles and especially on warm patios. In temperate climates, it is important to choose the best quality pots, because poorly fired terra-cotta is not frost hardy, and will crack in a severe or prolonged frost.

Concrete is usually seen in the form of classical containers and urns, useful in historical recreations or large country houses. Care should be taken in a small garden where an inappropriate design may look a little incongruous.

Plastic copies of terra-cotta and lead containers are difficult to distinguish from the real thing, and the advantage is that plastic is a light material – ideal for roof or balcony gardens. The disadvantage of plastic containers is that the soil in them dries out more quickly and they do not weather as well. If you use other types of

Free-standing and hanging baskets made from plastic-coated wire and painted cast iron.

plastic containers, remember that the container should not be the focus of attention, but rather it should be used to show off the plants, so choose a subdued color. Many are a bright white, and these can be dealt with by painting dark green.

Wooden containers, which come in many different types, from the traditional Versailles tub to a wooden barrel cut in half, need careful placing. They may not be suitable for some locations – in a country garden or on a farmhouse porch are, perhaps, the most appropriate.

Metal containers of all kinds can be used as long as they can hold soil. Lead urns and containers are a good choice for a period garden. Those available are mainly antique, but good copies are now commercially available.

Glazed pots and containers are available in a variety of shapes and sizes, often with an oriental design. Use them with caution because too bold a pattern on their side will detract from the plants.

Plants for glazed containers must be chosen with care. This Japanese maple, Acer palmatum *"Dissectum," is the perfect choice for this container.*

Tools

A small **gardener's trowel** is all that you need to dig holes ready for planting.

A **watering can** with a long neck is preferable. The longer the spout the better, since the flow of water is easier to control. A nozzle with fine holes is essential to give the plants a good drenching without damage. There is a wide range of watering cans available, from bright red plastic ones to green metal ones.

A **hose**, with a spray attachment, is useful when a large number of containers are involved. Some very good fine spray attachments are now available.

A **sealant gun** is essential for applying the waterproof sealant to cracks and holes in containers when creating a water garden (see the project on page 38).

Feeding

With a good potting soil, there is no need to add fertilizer at planting time, but because watering washes many of the nutrients out of the soil, feeding as growth progresses is essential.

A **general liquid fertilizer** throughout the summer, every other day, will keep a display going and help winter- and spring-flowering plants to build up their strength. However, any arrangement that is to continue through the winter should not be fed in late summer and fall, since this encourages soft sappy growth, easily cut back by frost.

Controlled-release fertilizers in the form of tablets and capsules, which are pressed down into the soil at planting time, are effective over a long period, slowly releasing their nutrients into the compost.

Materials

Peat-based potting soil

Peat-based potting soil has always been the first choice for most containers. It has the advantage of being light and, therefore, ideal in hanging baskets, containers which are intended to be moved around, and in roof gardens or balconies. The disadvantage is that it dries out very quickly so plants growing in it must be watered frequently. However, peat is extracted from peat beds, and there has been much environmental damage. Some peat beds are now being managed, so the best approach would be to seek out a manufacturer with a sound environmental policy. There are also some alternative soils now appearing, based around shredded forest bark, and these would be an excellent choice.

Crockery shards are needed for drainage in the bottom of containers. The best are broken pieces of terra-cotta flowerpots, although broken tiles or medium-size stones collected from the garden would also suffice.

Moss is used to line hanging baskets. It is easily obtainable from garden centers; an alternative source is to use moss raked from the lawn, but you must make sure that no chemicals have been used to treat the grass.

Broken flowerpots make the best shards.

Coir, or coconut fiber, is sold as a viable alternative to peat; however, there is now a question mark over this because the soil in its native environment is being impoverished by its removal.

Moss

Soil-based potting soil, being very heavy, should only be used in containers which are permanently sited and not on roof gardens or balconies. It has the advantage of drying out more slowly.

Soil-based potting soil

Watering

A regular water regime is most important. The main reason for container plants failing is that they have not been watered sufficiently. In hot weather, they need watering twice a day: once in the morning and again in the evening. Continue watering until a puddle appears under the container, which may take a minute or two, depending on the size of the container.

Wind can have a serious drying effect, particularly on hanging baskets. In hot or warm windy weather, these containers will need watering three times daily: morning, early afternoon,

It is much easier to control the flow of water with a long spout on the watering can.

and evening. In severe weather, it would be best to remove the basket to a sheltered spot, returning it later when the weather becomes more clement.

In **normal weather** conditions, check the top of the soil with your finger, and only water the plant if it is not damp to the touch.

Care should be taken to avoid splashing water on the leaves because this can cause them to scorch in the sun.

Soil additives, which hold water and release it slowly to the plants, are useful if you are unable to water your plants for a day or two.

Garden Design

RICHARD KEY

Containers can add height and impact to a small sitting area.

Containers are useful tools for the designer, and growing plants in ornamental containers allows flexibility in layout and a variety of heights anywhere in the garden, as well as adding color and interest all year round.

Interest can be added to any garden, large or small, and planted containers are a quick way of "furnishing" the patio. They may be used in various ways, perhaps singly to enhance a specimen plant or as an eye-catching focal point; in pairs either side of a door or archway, or framing a view or flight of steps; sited in groups to create bold effects, or to link the house with the terrace and garden; or on the walls around the edge of a patio to create a bright view which is easy to maintain.

The **color** of container plants can transform the bleakest concrete corner into a green and refreshing oasis. On patios, steps, roof terraces, and even tiny balconies, the colors, scents, textures, and sometimes tastes provided by planted containers offer a soft, friendly, inviting environment. It only takes a little know-how and imagination to turn a large ceramic bowl, wooden trough, or "old" chimney pot into a blaze of color, which can be used as an

Containers need not be planted to be effective. This terra-cotta urn has been discreetly, but effectively, used in a border situation.

Where the local soil conditions are unfavorable to them, some plants are better grown in containers. This acid-loving azalea is much happier in a container with acid soil than in the local chalky soil.

attractive feature in a small garden or to cheer up a patio or balcony.

Some plants have a very spectacular, but short, flowering season and are very untidy for the rest of the year. Plants like lilies, herbs, and vegetables are best displayed when they are at their best, and then the bulbs kept until the next season. Other plants, like agapanthus, flower better in containers and should also only appear in high summer. Tender plants, like fuchsias and geraniums, will need frost protection in the winter, and in containers they can easily be moved to a warmer spot. This mobile form of gardening is an essential part of the gardener's repertoire. Acid-loving plants, like azaleas and rhododendrons, can be grown in containers, using ericaceous compost, where the prevailing soil is alkaline.

Hanging baskets and **wall baskets** are always eye-catching and provide a quick way of brightening up a wall or trellis, without taking up too much space. Planted with herbs or vegetables, and sited close to the kitchen door, they will serve a useful purpose, as well as an ornamental one.

An **all-year garden** can be created by planting evergreens in containers. Attractive arrangements can be created by combining shrubs, dwarf conifers, and perennials, with larger specimens planted in larger tubs, permanently placed. Interesting effects can be created by underplanting with a succession of bulbs, and bedding plants in summer, for color throughout the year.

Single containers can be placed with other plants to add color and interest.

SUMMER CASCADE

This spectacular way of growing plants, discovered in an old gardening book, is also an excellent way of growing herbs and alpines. Since it is to be viewed from one side only, a

cascade on either side of a doorway is a perfect way of enhancing bare walls, and one can be used very effectively as a centerpiece for a group of containers against a wall on a patio.

Materials

Five terra-cotta pots, one each of diameter 16½ inches; 14 inches; 10 inches; 7 inches; 5 inches

• Crockery shards • Peat-based or lightweight potting soil (so container is light to move)

QUICK TIPS

Planting time: spring   **Light:** sun

Care: it is important to keep the compost moist, so plants can draw water and nutrients from the reservoir of compost under each pot.

This scheme is made up of annuals and tender perennials, and will need replanting each spring. Bring the fuchsia and geraniums into a frost-free environment during the winter, since these plants are half-hardy.

Life expectancy: one summer season, but several years for the fuchsia and geraniums if protected from frost.

The Plants

The flowers of the fuchsia contrast delightfully with the pale or dark blue trailing lobelia and white sweet alyssum. The trailing pink-flowered geraniums trail down the sides of the pot to mingle with the trailing pink trumpet-shaped flowers of the petunias.

5 surfinia petunias (Petunia "Pink Mini")

1 Fuchsia "Winston Churchill"

AN ALTERNATIVE PLANTING

For a warm sunny spot, to give a striking one-color display throughout the summer, plant rosemary (*Rosmarinus officinalis* "Miss Jessopp's Upright") to replace the fuchsia; 3 red busy lizzies to replace the trailing lobelia, and 3 to replace the sweet alyssum; 3 red ivy-leaf geraniums to replace the geraniums, and 4 to replace the petunias. When the season is over, plant the rosemary out in the open ground.

6 white sweet alyssum (Lobularia maritima, previously known as Alyssum maritimum)

5 trailing lobelia (Lobelia erinus pendula)

6 ivy-leaf geraniums (Pelargonium "Little Gem")

1. Collect together the five differently sized containers. The traditional flowerpot shape is best because the rim adds stability to the arrangement.

2. Starting with the largest pot, cover the base of the pot with a generous layer of crockery shards to aid drainage.

3. Add sufficient compost to allow the next largest pot to sit inside the first comfortably. Make sure the compost is well consolidated for stability.

4. Holding the second container in place, add compost to the first in the space created between the two. Again make sure that the compost is pressed down firmly to hold the second pot in place. Continue in this way until all the pots are filled.

5. Starting at the top, plant the upright fuchsia in the smallest pot and the 5 trailing lobelia in the second layer. The 6 sweet alyssum in the third layer will grow through the trailing lobelia.

6. The 6 ivy-leaf geraniums in the fourth layer will grow through the lobelia and trail down the side of the container, where it will combine with the petunias. After planting, water thoroughly to help firm in the plants and remove any air pockets.

EVERGREEN FLOWERPOT

*B*y using evergreens, we can insure color in the container throughout the year. Here, we have used larger garden plants which will give a colorful display for many years before outgrowing the container and needing to be planted in the open ground. The pot should be brought in close to the house, or a path, where it can be enjoyed all the year round.

Materials

A terra-cotta pot, diameter 16½ inches • Crockery shards • Peat- or soil-based potting soil

QUICK TIPS

Planting time: spring or fall
Light: sun or shade

Care: if placed in a sunny position, the container will require watering at least once a day. In winter, it will require watering once a month and would benefit from some protection from frost in colder areas.
Life expectancy: the plants can stay in the pot for at least 3 years with an annual top dressing of compost. Eventually, when the plants become too large for the pot, they should be planted out into the garden.

The Plants

The *choisya*, with its scented white flowers in late spring and early summer followed by occasional blooms throughout the summer, has finely divided leaves, which are a good foil for many perennials and shrubs. Underneath, the variegated ivies and the periwinkles cascade down the sides of the container, the white variegation contrasting with the terra-cotta of the container and the azure blue flowers of the vinca in spring.

1 Choisya "Aztec Pearl"

3 periwinkles
(*Vinca minor* "Azurea Flore Pleno")

3 variegated ivies
(*Hedera helix* "Glacier")

1. Cover the base of the container with crockery shards to aid with drainage.

2. Fill the container to approximately 2½ inches below the rim to aid watering, making sure the compost is well consolidated. Plant the choisya in the center of the container.

3. Plant the 3 periwinkles, equally spaced around the outside of the container.

4. Finish the container with 3 ivies planted in the gaps between the vinca.

AN ALTERNATIVE PLANTING

This container has the added advantage of containing shade-loving plants. Plant 1 *Elaeagnus pungens* "Maculata" in place of the choisya, 3 *Liriope muscari* in place of the periwinkles, and 3 *Pachysandra terminalis* "Variegata" to replace the variegated ivies.

5. After planting, water thoroughly to firm up the soil. The finished container will quickly fill out, and will provide color from the moment it is planted up.

WINTER WINDOW BOX

A window box is perfect for brightening up any house. Try siting one at each window and planting each with an identical planting scheme. When the winter

pansies have finished, you could plant the box with trailing red ivy-leaf geraniums in the spring, to create a stunning effect in midsummer.

Materials

A window box about 30 inches x 6½ inches high x 8 inches deep • Crockery shards • Peat-based potting soil

QUICK TIPS

Planting time: spring
Light: sun or partial shade

Care: an occasional watering is all that will be necessary. Deadheading helps to keep a continuity of blooms.
Life expectancy: one winter season.

The Plants

Yellow winter-flowering pansies add a bright and cheerful splash of color all winter long.

GRAHAM A. PAVEY

*12 yellow winter flowering pansies
(Viola tricolor)*

1. First, if the bottom of the box has no drainage holes, drill one at each end, 2 inches in diameter. Cover the bottom of the box with a layer of shards and fill with peat-based potting soil to approximately 2½ inches from the top.

2. Plant the pansies close together until the whole box is filled. You will need 12 plants for a box this size.

3. After planting, water thoroughly.

4. Winter-flowering pansies will flower all winter, flowering even better after a very cold spell.

SPRINGTIME HALF-POT

Although mainly spring-flowering, this container has evergreen interest all the year round. It flowers from mid-fall to early

summer, and should be placed where it can be seen during that period, near a frequently used path or doorway.

Materials

1 terra-cotta half-pot 14½ inches x 9 inches • Crockery shards • Peat-based potting soil

QUICK TIPS

Planting time: fall, or when potted daffodils are obtainable
Light: sun or shade

Care: after the daffodils have finished flowering, the leaves help to build up the store of food in the bulb for flowering the following year, so this is a good time to liquid feed. The leaves should be allowed to die down naturally. When they have turned brown, remove them from the plant.

Throughout the summer months, water daily in hot weather and feed once a week with liquid fertilizer. Do not neglect it during its dormant season.
Life expectancy: the laurustinus is a large garden plant and will outgrow the container in a couple of years, when it should be planted out into the garden. At this point, replant the arrangement.

The Plants

The laurustinus, one of the longest flowering shrubs, flowers from fall through to mid-spring when the daffodils are then at their best, and the evergreen white rock cress is starting to flower from late spring to early summer.

AN ALTERNATIVE PLANTING

Plant a *Prunus lusitanica* "Variegata" in the center of the container, surrounded by 8 *Narcissus* "Thalia" and 12 *Aubretia deltoidea*.

1 laurustinus (Viburnum tinus)

8 daffodils (Narcissus "Jack Snipe")
A small yellow daffodil

12 rock cress (Arabis caucasica)
A gray-leaved low-growing rock plant with white flowers in early summer

1. Place shards in the bottom of the container and add potting soil. Plant the laurustinus in the center, with the top of the rootball about 2½ inches lower than the top of the pot.

2. Add soil to just below the top of the laurustinus rootball. Plant the 8 daffodil bulbs, equally spaced around the edge of the rootball, with the base of each bulb being about 6 inches below the top of the soil. Take care to insure each bulb is the right way up.

3. Bring the potting soil up to the top of the rootball, firming gently, and plant the 12 rock cress around the perimeter, to cascade down the side of the container.

4. After planting, give the container a good watering to help firm in the plants. The arrangement will start to make a contribution quite quickly, and can be placed in its position immediately.

5. In spring, the daffodils will be at their best, the laurustinus will still be flowering, and the rock cress will be starting to flower. The leaves of the daffodils should be allowed to die down naturally.

6. In summer, the daffodils will have died down, but the rock cress will take over until later in the season, while the laurustinus will provide height and stability.

SUMMERTIME STONE TROUGH

Classical stone troughs of this size and shape can be difficult to plant up successfully. The final result of this project is subtle, but very *effective, and especially so, sited on top of a low wall with a collection of containers grouped around the base of the wall.*

Materials

A stone trough, about 32½ inches x 10½ inches high x 11½ inches deep • Crockery shards • Soil-based potting soil

QUICK TIPS

Planting time: spring
Light: sun or partial shade

Care: in hot weather, two waterings a day will be necessary; otherwise, one watering, first thing in the morning, should be sufficient. Feed with a liquid fertilizer every week.

The plants will need replanting on an annual basis. For winter color, remove these plants in the fall and replace with winter-flowering pansies.
Life expectancy: one summer season.

AN ALTERNATIVE PLANTING

Plant 12 blue lobelia (*Lobelia erinus*) to replace the sweet alyssum; 12 phlox (*Phlox drummondii*) to replace the verbenas;
9 tobacco plants (*Nicotiana* "Dwarf White Bedder") to replace the petunias; and 9 begonias (*Begonia semperflorens*) to replace the busy lizzies.

1. Plant up the container in its flowering position since it is very heavy and difficult to move.

Cover the bottom of the container with a layer of shards, and cover this with a layer of potting soil to approximately 2½ inches from the top. The extra weight of a soil-based potting soil will have little effect on an already-heavy container.

The Plants

White-centered red and pink flower clusters of verbenas, pink and mauve trumpets of petunias, and white sweet alyssum mingle with bright busy lizzies to provide a brilliant splash of color as summer unfolds, until the first frosts.

12 sweet alyssum (Lobularia maritima, previously known as Alyssum maritima)

12 verbenas (Verbena hybrida "Showtime")

9 petunias (Petunia hybrida)

9 busy lizzies (Impatiens "Elfin Mix")

2. Start by planting the busy lizzies, equally spaced around the container.

3. Tap each plant out of its container, and tease out the roots before planting to encourage quick new growth.

4. Fill in around the busy lizzies with the remaining plants, keeping the sweet alyssum close to the edge.

GARDEN MATTERS

5. Water thoroughly after planting to remove any air pockets.

6. The plants will grow away quickly, and the container will begin to contribute to the garden immediately.

SHADY CORNER HALF-POT

*A*lthough flowering in the winter, this arrangement has all-year-round interest and is perfect in a shady corner. Sweet box has a delightful vanilla scent which fills the air in midwinter, lifting the spirit. It needs careful placing to be enjoyed to the full, ideally near a north-facing doorway with a little shelter from the wind to allow the scent to fill the air.

Materials

1 terra-cotta half-pot about 14½ inches x 9 inches • Crockery shards • Peat-based potting soil

AN ALTERNATIVE PLANTING

This gold and purple arrangement needs similar conditions to the main plan, and will also be at its best in the winter. Plant 1 Mexican orange blossom (*Choisya ternata* "Sundance") to replace the sweet box; 3 bergenias (*Bergenia* "Ballawley Hybrid"); 3 lilyturf (*Liriope muscari*) to replace the ferns; and 3 golden creeping jennie (*Lysimachia nummularia* "Aureum") to replace the ivies.

1 sweet box
(*Sarcococca humilis*)

The Plants

Delightfully scented sweet box is surrounded by heartleaf bergenias, with their large, round, leathery leaves and pink flowers in spring. Soft-shield ferns, with their tall, feathery evergreen fronds, and variegated ivies add a light touch.

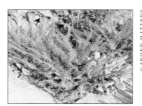

3 soft-shield ferns
(*Polystichum setiferum*)

3 heartleaf bergenias
(*Bergenia cordifolia*)

3 variegated ivies
(*Hedera helix* "Glacier")

1. Line the base of the container with shards and fill with soil to within 2½ inches of the rim. Plant the main plant, a sweet box, in the center.

2. Plant 3 soft-shield ferns equally spaced around the edge. The divided leaves of this plant will add a soft touch to the arrangement.

3. Plant the heartleaf begonias equally spaced between the ferns. The round leaves contrast well with the other elements in the pot.

4. Finish off with the three ivies planted to cascade down the side of the container, their white variegation contrasting well with the red terra-cotta.

5. After planting, water thoroughly to consolidate the arrangement and remove any air pockets. The scheme will develop quite quickly and can be used immediately.

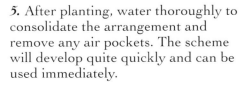

WINTER PYRAMID

A slow-growing conifer is an ideal subject for use in a container, not outgrowing it for several years. This arrangement is perhaps best placed

as a single container for a focal point, or on the corner of a path or beside a doorway. In the summer months, purple petunias could replace the pansies.

Materials

1 terra-cotta cylinder pot 15 inches diameter x 11 inches high
• Crockery shards • Peat-based potting soil

1. Line the base of the container with crockery shards. Add soil to a level where the conifer sits comfortably, the top of its rootball 2½ inches lower than the rim. Remove the plant from its container by inverting it, squeezing the sides, and gently encouraging it out. Tease out the roots, and plant in the center of the arrangement.

QUICK TIPS

Planting time: fall
Light: better in full sun, but will grow in shade

Care: apart from replanting the pansies each year, the arrangement will need little attention. Conifers are thirsty, however, and need regular watering throughout the summer – two or three times a day if in an exposed position. Feed with a liquid fertilizer each week from spring through to midsummer.
Life expectancy: the conifer can remain in the container for up to five years or more, if the top layer of soil is replaced each spring. Replant the pansies each year, and the ivies every two or three years.

The Plants

Usually grown as single specimens, because they die back where other plants grow against them, conifers appear very formal. The answer is to grow annuals and bedding plants at their base, which are removed before any permanent damage can be done. Here, distinctive, large, round-faced purple winter pansies contrast well with ivy and the golden conifer foliage.

1 Thuja occidentalis "Sunkist"

GRAHAM A. PAVEY

6 purple winter pansies (Viola tricolor)

5 variegated ivies (Hedera helix "Glacier")

2. Plant the ivies equally spaced around the edge to grow down the side of the container.

3. Infill with the pansies. After planting, water thoroughly to consolidate the roots, before placing it in position in the garden.

4. As the scheme develops, it will form a pyramid shape with the ivies eventually hiding the container.

SUMMER HANGING BASKET

Hanging baskets have become very popular, with an industry growing up around them. Nurseries compete to produce new and unusual plants to grow in them, and manufacturers find new ways of watering them. This hanging basket is very traditional and  *a proven favorite, offering a high degree of success. Almost as successful are begonias (Begonia semperflorens) planted instead of busy lizzies. Hanging baskets can be very effective if suspended from the crosspieces along the side of a pergola.*

1. Press moss into the base of the basket, bringing it up the sides to the level where the first layer of plants will be added.

2. Plant 4 busy lizzies, equally spaced around the basket. Squeeze the root-balls, as necessary, to push them between the wires.

Materials

A hanging basket, 14 inches in diameter • Moss • A sheet of plastic • Peat-based potting soil

The Plants

Busy lizzies are also happy growing in shade, although the arrangement will become more open as they grow.

*12 busy lizzies
(Impatiens "Elfin Mix")*

3. Cut out a circle from the plastic (the soil bag would be a perfect source). Make three holes in it to insure the potting soil is kept moist, but not waterlogged, and place it on the bed of moss in the bottom of the basket.

4. Build the moss up the side of the container to the next level of planting, and plant 4 more busy lizzies between those already planted.

5. Add more moss, bringing it up to 2½ inches above the top of the basket to create a "dish" in the center, and thereby aid watering. Fill the center with potting soil, firming and consolidating the plants and moss around the perimeter.

6. Finish the container by planting 4 busy lizzies in the top, and water well to consolidate the plants.

7. The finished container can be used immediately, although it should not be exposed to frost and may be better grown on in a greenhouse until all danger has passed.

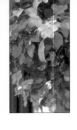

GARDEN MATTERS

8. As the season unfolds, the basket will
fill out to form a complete ball of color.

SUMMER WALL BASKET

*O*ld hay racks, originally used for feeding livestock, make ideal planting containers, but newly manufactured versions are, perhaps, the easiest to obtain.
A single basket can look a little lost, so it is a good idea to use several, equally spaced on a long wall, with a similar planting in each.
An ideal place to grow herbs, a basket of this nature could be installed in the kitchen, handy to the cook, placed close to a window to give it plenty of light.

Materials

A wall basket, 16 inches in diameter •
Moss • A sheet of plastic
• Peat-based potting soil

QUICK TIPS

Planting time: spring   **Light:** full sun

Care: as with all baskets, drying out is its biggest enemy. Keep well watered, especially in hot and windy conditions when three waterings a day will be required. Under normal conditions, water in the morning and again in the evening, and feed with a liquid fertilizer every other day.
Life expectancy: one summer season.

AN ALTERNATIVE PLANTING

Plant a trailing fuchsia to replace the ivy-leaf geranium; and a zonal geranium to replace the upright fuchsia. Plant 4 white trailing lobelia to replace the blue trailing lobelia; 3 white sweet alyssum to replace the busy lizzies; 3 lobelia to replace the verbenas; and a creeping jennie (*Lysimachia nummularia*) to replace the catnip.

The Plants

Pink, red, and white verbenas, busy lizzies, and an upright fuchsia combine with trailing catnip, blue lobelia, and a pink ivy-leaf geranium.

3 verbenas (Verbena hybrida "Showtime")

3 busy lizzies (Impatiens "Elfin Mix")

1 upright fuchsia. Fuchsias have bell-shaped flowers of red, pink, purple, and white all summer

4 trailing lobelia (Lobelia erinus pendula)
A trailing plant with pale or dark blue flowers

1 ivy-leaf geranium
(Pelargonium peltatum "Abel Carriere")

1 trailing catnip (Nepeta hederacea)

27

1. Place a layer of moss across the bottom of the container to make sure the contents do not fall out between the bars, and to hold moisture like a sponge. Cut a circle of plastic from the sheet or soil bag, make three holes in it, and place it on top of the moss. The plastic will help to maintain the moisture level, and the holes will insure that the compost does not become waterlogged.

2. Bring the moss up to the desired level for planting the "side" plants in a thin layer of soil – about halfway up the container. Carefully insert the rootball of the ivy-leaf geranium through the bars – if necessary, squash the rootball to gain access. Plant the 4 trailing lobelia in the same way.

3. Continue to add moss, carefully consolidating it around the roots of the plants already planted. Finish the moss off at about 2½ inches above the rim of the basket to create a hollow to aid watering.

4. Add a layer of compost, and plant the fuchsia in the center of the basket.

5. Plant the 3 busy lizzies and 3 verbenas around the fuchsia, and a single trailing catnip plant on one side. This vigorous plant will trail down to the ground and looks better planted alone on one side of the container.

6. The final container will require two screws or nails attached to a wall or fence for hanging. When planted, the container will make a contribution to the garden immediately.

7. Water well after planting to consolidate the arrangement. As the container develops, it will fill out, forming a large ball which, with careful attention, will flower throughout the summer.

WINTER HANGING BASKET

When the summer basket has finished, there is no need to store it away until the following spring — why not plant it up for the winter? This arrangement uses evergreens and could be maintained throughout the year; *although it may appear a little dull in the summer. Hang it close to a frequently used north-facing door or path, where its scent and sight can be enjoyed all winter.*

Materials

A hanging basket, 14 inches in diameter • Moss • A sheet of plastic • Peat-based potting soil

---

QUICK TIPS

Planting time: fall
Light: partial shade

Care: water sparingly throughout the winter, when the compost feels dry to the touch. Because of the checkerberries, only rainwater should be used.
Life expectancy: about two years. After this, move the plants to the open ground and replant the container.

AN ALTERNATIVE PLANTING

This scheme requires similar conditions, but it will not be necessary to water with rainwater. Plant 1 Alexandrian laurel (*Danae racemosa*) to replace the sweet box, and 2 carpet bugles (*Ajuga reptans* "Atropurpurea") to replace the thymes. Plant 2 saxifrages (*Saxifraga moschata* "Cloth of Gold") to replace the violas; 2 creeping jennies (*Lysimachia nummularia*) to replace the ivies; and 2 *Sisyrinchium bellum* to replace the checkerberries.

The Plants

The vanilla-scented flowers of the sweet box can be enjoyed in midwinter, while the acid-loving checkerberries will colonize the top of the soil and even hang over the edge. The red berries contrast with the flowers of the violas and the variegated colors of the ivy.

2 violas (Viola labradorica)

*1 sweet box
(Sarcococca humilis)*

*2 wooly thymes
(Thymus pseudolanuginosus)*

*2 checkerberries
(Gaultheria procumbens)*

*2 variegated ivies
(Hedera helix* "Glacier")

1. Build up the container using the same method as for the summer basket (see page 28). Plant the 2 wooly thymes and 2 violas alternately in the side of the basket.

2. Plant the sweet box in the center. Plant the variegated ivies to hang over the edge.

3. Finish the arrangement with the 2 checkerberries planted in between the ivies.

4. Water thoroughly with rainwater to remove any air pockets. The basket will take a few weeks to fill out, and may need some encouragement in a cool greenhouse.

HERB FLOWERPOT

Herbs in containers can be placed close to where they are needed, and this arrangement has been designed to be ornamental as well as functional, offering all-year-round interest. This container is the perfect choice as the central feature in a group of three: a rosemary in a medium-size container and a sage in a smaller one placed in front of it. The whole group looks good in the corner of a warm sunny patio.

Materials

A terra-cotta flowerpot, 16½ inches in diameter
• Crockery shards • Peat-based potting soil

QUICK TIPS

Planting time: spring, ideally, or as required
Light: sun or partial shade

Care: each morning check the soil for moisture with a fingertip, and only water if dry.
Life expectancy: the finished scheme can be left untouched for approximately two years before any serious maintenance will be required. At this time, it would be best to remove the lower planting, add some fresh soil, and replant.

AN ALTERNATIVE PLANTING

Plant a rosemary (*Rosmarinus officinalis* "Miss Jessopp's Upright") to replace the bay; 3 gold-splashed oregano (*Oreganum vulgare* "Gold Tip") to replace the thyme; 3 chives (*Allium schoenoprasum*) (there are no substitutes for chives); and 3 thymes (*Thymus serpyllum* "Annie Hall") to replace the creeping jennie.

The Plants

Herbs are perfect plants for container-growing. Many come from hot, dry countries, and the oil in their leaves, which gives their aroma and taste, evaporates more slowly than water, allowing them to cope with neglect better than other plants.

1 bay (Laurus nobilis)

GRAHAM A. PAVEY

3 creeping jennie (Lysimachia nummularia)

3 chives (Allium schoenoprasum)

3 lemon thyme (Thymus × citriodorus "Variegata")

1. Place a layer of crockery shards in the bottom of the container and add compost. Remove the main plant, a bay, from its pot by inverting it and gently squeezing, or tapping, until the rootball drops out. Tease out the roots to prepare it for planting. Add potting soil to a level where the plant sits comfortably, the top of its rootball 2½ inches lower than the rim of the container. Fill around the plant with potting soil, firming as you go, up to the top of the rootball.

2. Plant the 3 thymes evenly spaced around the edge. The variegated leaves of this plant will be enhanced by the backdrop of the bay leaves, and will stand out well against the terra-cotta.

3. Creeping jennie can become a nuisance when grown in the open ground. In a container, it can be allowed to grow down the side and is easily controlled by the occasional trim. Plant 3 around the edge, one next to each thyme.

4. Shape and texture are an important element of planting design, and containers are no exception to these rules. Chives are the only herb with an upright, spiky texture, and they will add impact to the arrangement.

5. Water the container well after planting, and allow a month before harvesting the herbs. It offers immediate interest, and the chive flowers begin to appear in late spring and early summer.

SUMMER WOODEN HALF-BARREL

Half-barrels can be difficult to plant up effectively, but this scheme makes an attractive summer planting simply by using two varieties of plants. One on either side of a warm, sunny doorway would be the perfect choice.

Because this is a scheme for summer, and the container may be difficult to move, it is a good idea to dig up and overwinter these tender perennials in a frost-free place. Replant the container for winter color when the summer display has finished.

Materials

A half-barrel, about 14 inches high x 20 inches diameter • Crockery shards • Peat- or soil-based potting soil

QUICK TIPS

Planting time: spring   **Light:** full sun

Care: the arrangement will need watering twice a day in very hot weather, but in normal conditions, once first thing in the morning. Feed with a liquid fertilizer twice a week to keep the flowers coming.

These perennial plants can be grown through the winter in a frost-free sunroom or porch. Otherwise, reduce the watering to once a month and bring the container into a frost-free shed or outbuilding to overwinter. If the container is a permanent fixture, remove all the plants and overwinter them separately.

Life expectancy: if winter protection is provided and some of the compost is replaced each spring, this container will give enjoyment for several years.

The Plants

Small bell-shaped flowers adorn the abutilon, and the trailing ivy-leaf geraniums are soon covered with pink flowers to fill the container to overflowing all summer long.

1 abutilon
(Abutilon "Kentish Belle")

GRAHAM A. PAVEY

8 pink ivy-leaf geraniums
(Pelargonium peltatum)

AN ALTERNATIVE PLANTING

This alternative planting, for winter color, uses a standard *Euonymus* "Silver Queen" to replace the abutilon, and 16 red winter pansies to replace the geraniums.

1. Spread a layer of crockery shards across the base of the half-barrel, and fill with potting soil. Use soil-based if the container is to remain where it is permanently, and peat-based if it is to be moved around. Remove the abutilon from its pot by inverting it and squeezing the sides. Gently tease out the roots before planting it toward the back of the container. Leave any supporting stake on to give the plant height.

2. Plant geraniums to fill up the rest of the container. Remove any supporting sticks to allow the plants to trail.

3. Water well after planting, and grow the container on in a frost-free place, moving it outside when all danger of frost has passed. If the container is permanently placed, do not plant up until the danger of frost has passed.

4. The container will flower the whole summer through, the geraniums quickly covering the wooden sides.

HYACINTH BOWL

*B*owls of this nature look good when planted as small alpine gardens or with a single variety of bulb, such as bright red tulips (Tulipa praestans "Fusilier"). This project uses a single variety of hyacinths to create a

spectacular effect in spring. It is effective on the corner of a patio or path, or in a group of three on a large patio. Three bowls of different sizes, each planted with a different single color, make a fine group.

Materials

A raised bowl, about 20 inches x 8 inches • Crockery shards • Peat-based potting soil

The Plants

These beautiful bright blue hyacinths will flower in early to mid-spring. A chemical in the bulb can irritate the skin, so use gloves when handling them, or protect your hand with a plastic bag.

20 hyacinth bulbs
(Hyacinthus orientalis "Amethyst")

1. Place a layer of crockery shards in the bottom to cover the drainage hole.

2. Fill with potting soil to 4 inches below the top of the container. Press the 20 bulbs gently into the compost, evenly spaced around the bowl. Use a peat-based soil because this container will need moving out of sight when it has finished flowering.

QUICK TIPS

Planting time: fall
Light: shade or partial shade

Care: feed with a liquid fertilizer when the plants have finished flowering, and allow the leaves to die down naturally. Water occasionally throughout the summer.
Life expectancy: indefinite, as long as the maintenance regime is followed.

3. Finally, cover the bulbs and bring the level of compost up to 2½ inches below the rim of the bowl.

4. After planting, water thoroughly to settle the compost. Overwinter the bulbs in a cool greenhouse or shed.

WATER GARDEN

A container can be the perfect way to create a water garden where space is limited. It can look most effective as the central feature of an arrangement, surrounded with containers of plants, such as grasses, bamboos, and hostas. The container could be sunk into the ground to create a water garden that is perfect for wildlife and makes an unusual addition to a flower border.

Materials

A container 15 inches high x 20 inches diameter • Waterproof sealant

• Sealant gun • 3 engineering bricks

• Gravel or small granite chips

• 3 pieces of broken flowerpot or tile

QUICK TIPS

Planting time: spring
Light: sun or partial shade

Care: although the plants are hardy, it is best to give some winter protection, because expanding ice may damage the container.

The marginal plants (iris and marsh marigold) may need planting into larger plastic pots in time. Use a plastic basket available at a water-garden specialist and a proprietary water-garden soil or garden loam – ordinary potting soil will add too many nutrients to the water and encourage algae. There are chemicals available which keep the algae under control, and these should be added to the water, as long as livestock is not to be introduced.
Life expectancy: with the occasional tidy and repotting of the plants, this water feature should last for many years.

The Plants

It is important to select a dwarf water lily. A plant such as *Nymphaea alba* is a monster, only suitable for large ponds or lakes. Many water plants are quick colonizers, unsuitable for small containers, so careful selection is important.

*1 marsh marigold
(Caltha palustris "Plena")*

1 water lily (Nymphaea)

*1 Japanese iris (Iris ensata "Variegata")
(also known as Iris kaempferi "Variegata")*

1. To make sure the container holds water, seal any holes and cracks with a waterproof sealant – the substance used for sealing around window frames. Apply a circle of sealant around each drainage hole, making sure that the contact area is clean beforehand.

2. Cover sealant with a piece of flowerpot or broken tile, pressed into place. Allow 24 hours for this to dry before adding water.

3. Add a layer of gravel. Use bricks as plinths for the plants to make sure they are sitting at the right height.

4. Place the plants, in their pots, on the bricks or gravel in the container. For the iris and marsh marigold, the top of the soil should be just below the surface of the water. The water lily should be deeper, sitting on the gravel, but it must be lowered in stages. Start it off at a level where the leaves float comfortably on the surface, then lower it slowly week by week as new growth appears. Adjust the plant height by adding or removing the gravel and bricks. Fill with water to the desired level. Keep the end of the hose under the water to reduce damaging turbulence.

AN ALTERNATIVE PLANTING

Half-barrels are perfect for this type of project. Seal the cracks between the slats with sealant to create a waterproof container. Plant this selection of less-invasive water plants: a sweet flag (*Acorus calamus* "Variegatus") to replace the iris; a water forget-me-not (*Myositis scorpioides*) to replace the marsh marigold; and a water lily (*Nymphaea* "Hermine").

5. If planted in the spring, a succession of color will start almost immediately with the yellow flowers of the marsh marigold and purple flowers of the iris, followed by water lilies in the summer.

CHIMNEY POT

*O*rnate terra-cotta chimney pots should not be overlooked as attractive and interesting plant containers. They look a little self-conscious and awkward if displayed alone, but one is effective as the focal point of a large group, or placed in a mixed border where the plants can grow around it.

Materials

A chimney pot • Crockery shards • Peat- or soil-based potting soil

The Plants

Trailing plants and ground-cover roses are good choices for chimney pots because the plants will cover the stark body but leave the more interesting top exposed. Climbers are a good choice, but most would be too large for such a small amount of soil. However, the smaller clematis is a perfect choice.

1 Clematis "Helsingborg"

1. The size of the chimney pot is not important. Place crockery shards in the bottom, and fill with soil to the base of the castellations. Here, a terra-cotta copy has been used. For real chimney pots, place a suitable plastic flowerpot in the bottom of the container to act as a base. If the chimney pot is tall, partially fill with rubble to reduce the amount of compost required.

3. Clematis should be planted at least 8 inches lower than the top of the rootball, so it will rejuvenate from below the surface if attacked by clematis wilt, an airborne fungus, which can otherwise kill young plants. Add potting soil to bring the level up to 2½ inches below the base of the castellation.

2. Remove the clematis from the flowerpot by inverting it, squeezing the sides, and gently easing out the rootball. Tease out the roots before planting.

4. Untie the plant from the supporting cane to allow it to cascade over the edge of the container.

QUICK TIPS

Planting time: early spring
Light: sun or shade

Care: feed with a liquid fertilizer in April to encourage flowering, and then feed monthly throughout the summer only. Do not neglect the watering during the summer when it is not in flower. It will require watering each day during hot weather, like any other container.
Life expectancy: even small clematis have a limited life in a small container. Replace after three years.

5. If the chimney pot is small, like this one, place it on a plinth, or on top of a low wall, to allow the climber room to develop.

CIRCULAR GROUP FOR SUN

Containers dotted randomly around the flower garden are not being used to their best advantage. Simply placing them together in a group is instantly more attractive. The easiest changes in a garden are often the most effective, such as the grouping of one large, one medium, and one small container in decreasing circles. Urns can often look good even without plants.

Materials

Five mixed-size containers • a large container, 11inches in diameter • Crockery shards • Peat-based potting soil

1. Placing containers in rows is a common way to display them. This semicircular group is most effective on the top of a wall, or on a large windowsill. On a patio, it may be less effective because it may form a barrier.

2. The pink and red zonal geraniums, the *Campanula* "G. F. Wilson," and the *Helichrysum petiolare* look better pulled together into a group, but still lack a focal point and height.

3 zonal geraniums, 2 red and 1 pink

1 Helichrysum petiolare

The Plants

Strong, bright colors in patio container plants are important when the sun is high. The campanula bears clusters of lavender or pale blue flowers in summer, which provide contrast to the striking geraniums. The group is further lifted by the softness of the helichrysum. The New Zealand cabbage palm suggests a cooling fountain. Spiky plants create interesting effects when their shadows come in to play.

1 Campanula "G. F. Wilson"

1 New Zealand cabbage palm (Cordyline australis)

3. A few spiky plants can make all the difference. Try adding groups of iris to an uninteresting mixed border. In this case, a New Zealand cabbage palm adds a central feature and sudden impact to a "flat" scheme.

QUICK TIPS

Planting time: spring   **Light:** sun

Care: each morning check the soil for moisture, and only water if dry. The campanula may require two or three waterings daily in hot weather.

Life expectancy: All the plants used are perennials, and may remain in their containers for many years if kept in a frost-free environment.

DESERT PLANT GROUP

*W*ell, perhaps not a desert, but certainly for a hot, dry sunroom or patio. The plants used are all sun-lovers, and will require protection from frost. This is the perfect choice for a Spanish- or Mexican-style garden where the temperatures are very high, there is little water, and few plants will grow.

Materials

Five terra-cotta pots, one each of 10 inches diameter x 7 inches high; 7½ inches diameter x 7 inches high; 7½ inches x 6 inches; and two 8 inches x 4 inches dishes • Crockery shards • Soil-based potting compost • Sharp gravel

QUICK TIPS

Planting time: at any time of the year
Light: full sun

Care: this scheme will tolerate neglect. In normal conditions, water once a week in summer, but not at all during the winter months.
Life expectancy: the plants can be kept in their containers for several years, and will only need attention if they outgrow their pots.

The Plants

This grouping of plants emphasizes the sharp outlines of the cacti family. The tiny white hairs that cover the houseleeks give the impression of a spider's web, contrasting with the bold, spiky mother-in-law's tongue. Echeveria, a low-growing succulent, will produce orange and yellow flowers in early summer, bringing a sprinkling of color to this unusual display.

*1 mother-in-law's tongue
(Sansevieria trifasciata)*

1 agave (Agave americana "Variegata")

1 cactus (Echinocactus grusonii)

5 echeverias (Echeveria derenbergii)

*5 cobweb houseleeks
(Sempervivum arachnoideum)*

1. Prepare each container by placing crockery shards over the drainage holes. Mix the sharp gravel with the soil, in the ratio 3 parts soil to 1 part gravel. Plant the largest container with the agave. This bold, spiky plant forms the centerpiece of the scheme. One of the two dishes is planted with the 3 echeverias, a low-growing succulent.

2. A globe-shaped cactus has been selected for the smallest container. Since the whole scheme lacks foliage and flowers, extremes in form have been chosen to add impact, and this globe shape contrasts well with the sword leaves of the agave.

AN ALTERNATIVE PLANTING

Plant a thread agave (*Agave filifera*) to replace the agave; a crassula (*Crassula socialis*) to replace the echeveria; an old lady cactus (*Mammillaria hahniana*) to replace the echinocactus; a pinwheel (*Aeonium haworthii*) to replace the houseleeks; and an organ pipe cactus (*Lemaireocereus marginatus*) to replace the mother-in-law's tongue.

3. These three containers make a good display on their own, but you can go further. Plant up the second dish with the 5 cobweb houseleeks. Plant the mother-in-law's tongue in the final container to give an upright dimension to the arrangement.

45

SHADE GROUP

This grouping would be perfect on a shady patio or in a cool north- or east-facing sunroom. Many town gardens and roof gardens, which are shaded by trees and taller buildings, have their whole planting scheme in containers. This grouping would be the perfect central feature in such a scheme. Try introducing a small upright statue into the group.

Materials

Five containers, one each of 20 inches diameter x 18 inches high; 16 inches x 12 inches high; 10 inches x 7½ inches; 12 inches x 9½ inches; 9 inches x 7 inches and 14 inches x 10 inches

QUICK TIPS

Planting time: at any time of the year
Light: partial or full shade

Care: it is essential that the soil in the containers is kept moist; although it is not necessary for all the plants, they will be much happier. It is best to use rainwater, because the pieris and the fetterbush prefer acid conditions.
Life expectancy: The bamboo, pieris, fetterbush, and baby's-tears will eventually outgrow their containers. Replanted into larger containers, they will be happy for an indefinite period. The hosta and astilbe will also outgrow their containers, but these can be divided and replanted.

The Plants

1 pieris (Pieris "Forest Flame")

1 hosta (Hosta sieboldiana "Elegans")

1 fetterbush (Leucothoe fontanesiana "Scarletta") Hanging, white pitcher-shaped flowers in spring

1 baby's-tears (Soleirolia soleirolii, also known as Helxine soleirolii) Tiny pale green leaves forming a mound

1 bamboo (Fargesia spathaceus, also known as Arundinaria murieliae)

1 astilbe (Astilbe "Peach Blossom")

1. The main plant in the group is a bamboo. Bamboos are excellent subjects for dry or damp shade, and perfect in large containers.

2. The next two plants in the group are moisture-loving and must not be allowed to dry out. The lower of the two is baby's-tears, whose tiny pale green leaves form a mound. It is often sold as a houseplant, but is perfectly hardy in the right conditions (in the garden it grows where it wants to grow, not where you want it to!). The larger plant is an astilbe, which is normally found in damp soil beside a pool, the tall, feathery pink flowers in early summer and the fern-like leaves contrasting well with so many other plants.

3. Pieris, which has white flowers in spring followed by bright red new growth, requires an acid soil and is usually found in a woodland garden (use an ericaceous compost for acid-loving plants).

4. To finish off the scheme, a fetterbush which has hanging white pitcher-shaped flowers in spring, and a hosta have been selected. The fetterbush, like the pieris, requires an acid soil. Its shape, and that of the hosta, add solidity to the design.

SUMMER STRAWBERRY POT

◦⬦◦

*O*riginally designed to grow strawberries, this terra-cotta container looks good planted with herbs beside the kitchen door, where they can be harvested for cooking.

*I*n a mixed border, it adds height and extra interest, and a group of three strawberry pots of different sizes, planted with a mix of plants, makes an excellent and unusual focal point for a

Materials

A strawberry pot 15 inches x 6½ inches • Crockery shards • Peat-based or lightweight potting soil (so container is light to move)

QUICK TIPS

Planting time: spring **Light:** full sun

Care: bring into a frost-free environment during the winter, because the plants used are half-hardy perennials.
Life expectancy: usually one summer, but several years if protected from frost.

1. Place a generous layer of crockery shards in the bottom of the pot. This will help drainage and stop the soil from falling through the drainage holes in the bottom of the container.

2. Fill the container with a peat-based or lightweight potting soil to the lowest holes on the side of the pot.

The Plants

2 Lotus berthelotii

4 polygonums
(Polygonum capitatum "Pink Bubbles")

The lotus, its gray leaves sprawling over the sides of the pot, contrasts well with the terra-cotta container and the variegated leaves and pink flowers of the polygonum, of similar habit. The rich blue flowers of trailing lobelia and a variegated scented-leaf geranium with tiny pink flowers completes the arrangement.

2 Lobelia "Kathleen Mallard"

1 scented-leaf geranium
(Pelargonium "Lady Plymouth")

3. Collect together all the plants you intend to use before starting to plant.

4. Plant 2 polygonums and 2 *Lotus berthelotii* in the first layer. To remove a plant, invert the plastic pot and gently squeeze its sides. Tease out the roots, and prepare the plant for planting.

5. Using both hands, carefully insert the plant into the container.

6. Add more potting soil, carefully consolidating it firmly around the plant roots. Bring the level up to the second layer of holes. Plant the next four plants: the 2 lobelia and 2 more polygonums.

7. Finally, the arrangement is finished off with the scented-leaf geranium.

AN ALTERNATIVE PLANTING

For a smaller strawberry pot, 12inches x 7inches, plant 3 trailing lobelia (*Lobelia erinus pendula*) in the first layer of holes; 3 strawberry plants in the second layer; and finish off the container with a trailing fuchsia (*Fuchsia* "Cascade").

The strawberries can remain in the container for three or four years, but the lobelia will need replacing each spring. The fuchsia is a tender perennial and must be brought into a frost-free place during the winter.

8. When planting is finished, water the container thoroughly.

FLOWER GARDENS

*Design stunning borders
to brighten up your garden from
season to season*

INTRODUCTION

GRAHAM A. PAVEY

GRAHAM A. PAVEY

GRAHAM A. PAVEY

F or a stunning border that brightens up the garden from season to season, and requires a low level of maintenance, planning is the key. By choosing plants carefully to make sure they suit the aspect, the soil, and are suitable companions for their neighbors, you can be certain of a changing display where there will nearly always be some attractive perennial to admire.

Constantly changing, the mixed border offers an annual tapestry of colors. Bulbs may dominate in spring, lush majestic flowers appear in summer, until the warm and rich colors of fall arrive with a flourish. In winter, a solid structure of evergreens creates all-year-round interest.

A modestly sized border can contain a mass of interesting plants. It should be located in a site where it can be enjoyed during its flowering season. A winter or spring border should be visible from the house, so you can get as much pleasure from it as possible. All you need is a sunny situation and a well-nourished soil that is not too heavy. Each project in this book offers a professionally designed border to the beginner, removing the doubt and insuring a successful display.

GRAHAM A. PAVEY

MATERIALS AND TECHNIQUES

Designing the Garden

Before looking at individual border projects, some thought should be given to the overall garden, and how simple design ideas can make a dramatic difference. The layout illustrated here is for a small and basic garden, but similar ideas could be used in any size of garden.

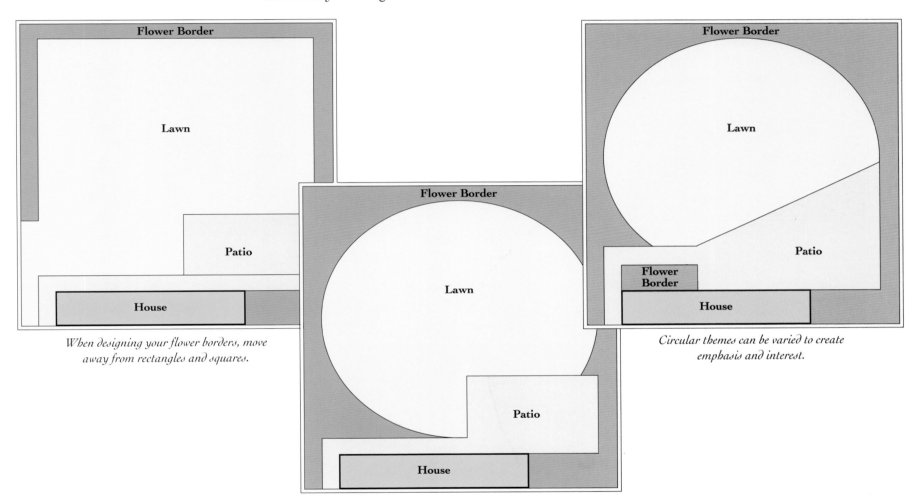

When designing your flower borders, move away from rectangles and squares.

Circular themes can be varied to create emphasis and interest.

Layout 1

Many new gardens have this kind of layout, with the house at one end and the garden behind it, often surrounded by a solid wooden fence. There may be a small patio close to the house and a rectangular lawn with a narrow border, around the perimeter of which unprepared soil is planted with whatever plants looked good at the garden center on the day of purchase.

Layout 2

First, try to forget about the rectangles and squares created by the site, and think of other shapes. Start by overlaying the garden with a circle. A circular lawn, for instance, will create large beds in each corner – borders with room to work in. The projects in this book could be used in any one of the corner beds created here.

Layout 3

By changing the angle of the patio, you can alter the whole emphasis of the garden, and push the sitting area out from the house to pick up more of the sun in north-, east-, and west-facing sites. The circular theme can now be "hung" off the patio and varied to suit the site.

Preparing the Ground

One of the keys to success is in the preparation of the soil – the more thoroughly the soil is improved, the better the final result. This preparation starts with digging in plenty of organic matter (see page 56, "Improving the Soil"), which generally comes in the form of compost or well-rotted animal manure, and sharp sand to lighten it and improve drainage. In a temperate climate where the soil has a clay content, the preparation is best carried out in the fall, and the soil left unplanted over the winter. This will allow the frost to work on it and break it down even more.

1. Dig out a trench across the whole width of the bed to one spade's depth. Place the surplus soil in a wheelbarrow, or to one side.

2. Line the base of the excavation with a 4 inch deep layer of organic matter; in this case, well-rotted horse manure.

3. Dig out a second trench beside the first.

4. Tip this surplus soil onto the organic matter in the first trench.

5. Line the new trench with organic compost, and repeat the cycle across the bed. When the bed has been completely dug over, fill the final trench with the soil removed from the original one.

6. After the ground has been prepared, or in the following spring, rake it to create a fine tilth for planting.

Soil Testing

Before deciding what preparation the soil needs, or what plants can be planted, the soil needs analyzing.

Acid or Alkaline

The first stage of this is to determine the pH of the soil, which indicates whether the soil is acid or alkaline. There are some plants, for instance, such as rhododendrons, most heathers, and azaleas, which need an acid soil and cannot grow in any other. Testing the pH of the soil can easily be done using a small kit available at any garden center. Follow the instructions on the test kit.

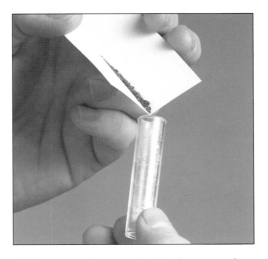

1. Place testing powder in the test tube to the first mark, and then add the soil to the second mark.

2. Fill the tube with *tap* water (the powder is balanced to accept alkaline tap water) and shake thoroughly.

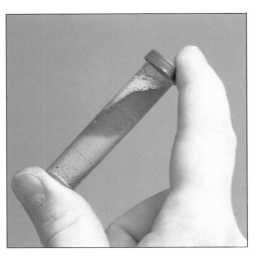

3. Leave the test tube to stand until the residue settles. With some soils, this may take a long time.

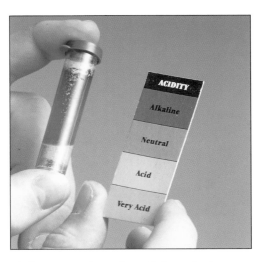

4. Compare the color of the solution with the accompanying color chart to determine the pH. This soil is alkaline.

If your soil is acid and you want to take advantage of the conditions, you might want to use the planting plan suggested for the Woodland Bed on page 93.

Soil Structure

After you have determined the pH of your soil, look at the soil structure. Take a walnut-size piece of soil, wet it, and attempt to roll it into a ball between the palms of your hands. If it keeps falling open with no adhesion at all, then the soil is a sandy one; if it can be formed into a smooth ball, then it is very heavy clay. Any form of ball indicates a clay content.

Sandy soils are open, free-draining, and low in nutrients because these are continually being washed from the soil. Improve this type of soil by digging in copious amounts of well-rotted organic matter, which acts as a sponge and holds in water and nutrients.

Clayey soils are difficult to work, but higher in nutrients. Improve clay soil by digging in organic material mixed with some form of sand or grit to improve drainage.

Improving the Soil

As well as well-rotted organic matter, there are other materials that can be incorporated into the soil, depending upon the conditions. Mix them in equal proportions with the well-rotted manure in Steps 1 to 5 on page 54, "Preparing the Ground."

Clayey soil can make life difficult in the garden. Being very slick in rainy weather and rock-hard in summer, it is difficult to work, having very tiny particles which cling tightly together. Because sand has large particles that are very open and do not cling together, the solution is to incorporate sand into the soil to open it up. The best sand for this is sharp sand, but any gritty material would be suitable, as long as it is clean.

Peat is a natural material obtained from peat bogs, and is excellent for conditioning the soil. Mixed in equal parts with manure or compost, it produces the very best material for preparing garden soil. Its removal has a detrimental impact on the natural environment, and it is recommended that if peat is to be used, only that extracted from managed sites should be used.

Coco-fiber or **coir** is a material that has been heralded as the revolutionary new alternative to peat, although it was in common use in the nineteenth century. From the environmental angle, there is a question mark over it, because it is said to be impoverishing the soil on the islands where it is found. Some environmentalists have now returned to using peat from managed sources. Use it in the same way as peat.

Loam is soil of medium texture that contains more or less equal parts of sand, silt, and clay, and is usually rich in humus. Where possible, improving the existing soil is always the best solution, but in some cases, where the soil is so poor, it is necessary to bring in a good-quality loam to replace the soil that already exists. Always ask for "screened" topsoil, because this has been treated to destroy any weeds or weed seeds. When the new soil is in place, it would still be best to dig the border as described in "Preparing the Ground."

Mulching

After the border has been planted, the secret of success is to keep the roots moist and cool throughout the summer. This can best be achieved by covering the soil around the roots when wet, in the spring, with a mulch. By eliminating light, it can also help to keep weeds down by preventing seeds from germinating and perennial weeds from growing.

Almost anything can be used as a mulch, from newspaper and old carpet to grass cuttings, but because the flower border is to be aesthetically pleasing, materials such as forest bark, pebbles, or mulching mats are recommended.

Forest bark is waste material from the logging and timber industry. It comes in several different grades, and is also used for soil conditioning and as a soft paving material in children's play areas. It must be 2 inches deep to be effective. Coco-fiber could be used as a viable alternative.

Mulch matting is an interwoven material, usually made of polypropylene, fiberglass, or a similar man-made material, and comes in a roll or as small squares or circles for individual plants. The weave allows water through to the soil, while still keeping weeds at bay.

Pea-size pebbles are very effective, but they immediately alter the character of the border and may influence the overall design of the garden, so care must be used when selecting.

Planting

Plants, like all living things, respond to thoughtful treatment. Care at planting time can pay dividends in the long run.

Dig a hole with a garden trowel, sufficient to take the whole rootball. Before planting, put the plant, in its pot, into the hole to make sure that the top of the soil in the pot is flush with the top of the surrounding soil. For holes for larger plants, use a spade.

When you remove the plant from its pot to plant it, you may find it has become "root-bound" in its pot. If planted in this state, any new roots will not invade the surrounding soil. It is, therefore, a good idea to gently "tease" out some of the roots before planting.

After planting, consolidate the soil around the roots by gently firming with the fingertips. With larger plants, use the heel of your shoe.

Plant Sizes

The size of the plant at the time of planting can be critical. If it is too small, it could be swamped by its neighbors before it has time to grow; too large, and it may initially be out of proportion with its neighbors. In the projects, the ideal pot size for each plant is indicated, but if these are difficult to obtain, then plants in larger pots would be acceptable.

Watering

After each plant has been planted, the roots should be given a good drenching from either a watering can or a gentle trickle from an open-ended hose. This will remove any air pockets from around the roots, as well as give the plant the water it needs for a good start.

Plant Protection

Some plants will require protection during a cold winter, and this is best done by covering them with plastic-foam cones, or by wrapping them up in burlap or a sheet of horticultural fiber, a "fleece" usually made of woven polypropylene.

Supporting Climbers

Most climbers will need some support to hold them against the structure chosen to accommodate them. Various methods may be employed, from plastic mesh to a solid wooden trellis, but the problem here is that the support is very visible and spoils the effect of the climber. The best solution is to use screw eyes and galvanized wire, which blend with the background and are virtually invisible. Attach three eyes, vertically and equally spaced, to each fence post, or about 6 feet apart on a wall.

Tools

A **spade** is an essential tool for preparing the border, either for edging or shoveling preparation materials. A smaller version, called a border spade, can be used for digging around existing plants without damage.

After the garden has been dug over, a **rake** can be used to smooth the surface, creating a fine tilth. Draw it backward and forward across the bed in different directions, breaking up any large lumps with a sharp slap, until the desired surface has been created.

A **gardener's trowel** is a useful small tool for digging small holes for planting.

A **hose** is needed once the border has been planted. Initially, watering helps to bed the plants in and remove any air pockets which may have developed while planting. Regular watering, especially in dry weather, will be essential to success. There are a number of excellent spray attachments now available, which gently water the plants without damage.

A **watering can** could be used for individual plants when planting up, and for close watering of individual plants that may need extra moisture.

A **wheelbarrow** is essential when preparing the ground for transporting manure, soil, gravel, or other materials to where it is needed.

Screw eyes provide support that blends into the background.

Galvanized wire is used with screw eyes for "wiring" a wall or fence to provide support for climbers.

Screw eyes are ideal for walls or screwing straight into a fence post, but you could also use masonry nails, which could be used in a fence post. Galvanized wire is fastened to the screw eyes to provide a network of wires to support climbing plants.

EAST-FACING CORNER BED

*D*ry, *with only direct sunlight in early morning, the east-facing border can cause problems, so plants which can cope with these conditions have been selected. For most of the year, this scheme relies*

on a variety of leaf shape and color, but from midsummer to fall the border will come to life with the crocosmia, which is followed by autumn leaf colors.

Tools

Spade • Garden trowel

The Plants

Astrantia major, 3½ inch or 5½ inch pot

2 *Crocosmia* "Lucifer," 3½ inch or 5½ inch pots

2 *Hebe rakaiensis,* 7½ inch pots

3 *Hosta sieboldiana* "Elegans," 5½ inch or 6½ inch pots

6 *Houttuynia cordata* "Chameleon," 3½ inch or 5½ inch pots

Lonicera japonica "Halliana," 7½ inch pot

Prunus lusitanica, 7½ inch pot

Vitis coignetiae, 7½ inch pot

QUICK TIPS

GRAHAM A. PAVEY

GRAHAM A. PAVEY

Astrantia major

Flowering season: the main season will be from midsummer to early fall.

Soil: any good garden soil.

Care: the laurel may require an annual prune to restrain it. Slug pellets placed around the hostas in the spring will deter snails and slugs from feasting on their leaves, although *H. sieboldiana* appears to be less palatable to them than other hostas. The climbers will need tying to the wires.

Crocosmia "Lucifer."

61

Planting Plan

STEP ONE
Main Structural Planting

The first plants to consider are the main evergreens and structural plants. Evergreens at each corner give the scheme balance and create all-year-round interest.

Prunus lusitanica (Portuguese laurel). This reliable evergreen will supply the main structure for this grouping. It has the advantage of growing anywhere, sun or shade, and flowers in early summer. It is a large plant, eventually forming a small tree. It can be pruned annually, once established, to keep it in check.

Vitis coignetiae (Crimson glory vine). This vine has large, round deciduous leaves, which turn crimson in the fall, and it is always an eye-catcher. The trunk becomes old and gnarled in time, giving a solid structure despite the lack of leaves in winter.

Hebe rakaiensis. Large-leaf hebes are, unfortunately, not reliably hardy in temperate zones, but those with smaller leaves are quite tough. This hebe has small, leaves and will form a small, solid mound, covered in white flowers during midsummer. It is the perfect plant for the corner of a bed, where it quickly establishes itself as a reliable structural plant.

Lonicera japonica "Halliana" (Honeysuckle). This evergreen climber will reliably smother any wall or fence as long as the structure is carefully "wired." It is not as fragrant as other honeysuckles, but compensates for that by providing a solid evergreen screen.

In-fill Planting

In a small bed or garden, it is useful to choose plants that offer "value for money," providing interest over a long period with attractive foliage, as well as flowers.

Astrantia major (Masterwort). With its attractive feathery foliage, which lasts all summer, and its rather curious cream-and-green flowers from mid to late summer, masterwort contrasts well with more solid shapes. Here, it is used as a foil for the hebe, the large leaves of the hosta, and the vine.

GRAHAM A. PAVEY

Hosta sieboldiana "Elegans" (Plantain lily). Hostas are excellent plants for associating with others. Their large, often variegated, leaves provide a foil for sword-shaped and feathery foliage. Most require shade and some moisture in the soil, but the *H. sieboldiana* varieties will cope with a dry soil and will even grow in full sun.

GRAHAM A. PAVEY

Houttuynia cordata "Chameleon". This marsh plant may spread freely through moist soil, becoming very invasive. It is one of the few plants which will grow in both boggy and dry conditions, and is much more restrained in dry soil. The unusual aromatic, pink, cream, and green variegated leaves offer interest throughout the summer, its white flowers being a bonus.

GRAHAM A. PAVEY

Crocosmia "Lucifer" (Montbretia). The sword-shaped leaves appear early in the season and contrast well with so many other plants. In late summer, the crocosmia adds its flame-red flowers to the scheme, where the astrantia will still be flowering. Combining with the houttuynia, it completely changes the character of the arrangement to become hot and vibrant, giving it a lift at a time when other plants are beginning to look a little tired.

GARDEN MATTERS

SOUTH-FACING CORNER BED

This aspect, in full sun for most of the day, gives the opportunity to grow sun-loving plants which may be difficult to grow elsewhere. Not all plants need full sun, so care must be taken to select plants *which enjoy these hot, dry conditions. A corner bed of this nature, facing south and backed by a wall or fence, could be planted up with bold hot colors to take advantage of the conditions.*

The Plants

Artemisia "Powis Castle," 7½ inch pot

Convolvulus cneorum, 7½ inch pot

Cotinus "Grace," 7½ inch pot

2 Geranium psilostemon, 3½ inch or 5½ inch pots

3 Osteospermum jacundum, 5½ inch or 6½ inch pots

4 Rosa "Little White Pet," 7½ inch pots or bare -rooted

3 Sisyrinchium striatum, 3½ inch or 5½ inch pots

2 Stachys olympica "Silver Carpet," 3½ inch or 5½ inch pots

2 Trachelospermum jasminoides, 7½ inch pots

Tools and Materials

Galvanized wire • Garden trowel • Spade • Screw eyes

QUICK TIPS

GRAHAM A. PAVEY

Geranium psilostemon

Flowering season: midsummer.

Soil: any garden soil. Heavy soil should be broken up with addition of sharp sand.

Care: the trachelospermums should be tied to the wires regularly. They must be protected in cold weather, perhaps using horticultural fiber or burlap, because severe windchill and frost will cut this plant back and may kill young specimens. Prune the smoke tree down hard each spring to encourage larger and more colorful foliage. The leaves of sisyrinchium blacken as they die, which is perfectly normal, but should be removed as soon as they appear. Cut the artemisia to within 4 inches of the ground each spring to maintain its shape.

Planting Plan

Main Structural Planting

Cotinus "Grace" (Smoke tree).
The large, purple leaves of this
deciduous shrub dictate the
overall color scheme of whatever
border it is planted in. Despite
being deciduous, the bare
branches have a solid shape,
contributing to the overall
framework.

Trachelospermum jasminoides. Like
an evergreen jasmine, this plant is
the perfect choice for a sheltered
wall. It must be protected in very
cold weather (see "Care").

Artemisia "Powis Castle." This is
a foliage plant which is perfect
for a myriad of uses. It is equally
at home with roses in a country
garden as it is with boxwood
hedges in a more formal setting.
It is important to cut the plant
back every spring to maintain its
shape.

Convolvulus cneorum. This silvery,
glistening relative of bindweed
needs careful placing in the
garden, because it must have full
sun or it will become untidy and
straggly.

In-fill Planting

Geranium psilostemon. This is the tallest growing of all hardy geraniums. When its bright magenta flowers appear in midsummer, it is like welcoming an old friend who only visits once a year. The geraniums seem to change color when viewed with the purple leaves of the smoke tree in the background, giving them an almost luminescent quality.

Stachys byzantina "Silver Carpet" (Lamb's-ears). This is a non-flowering variety, grown for its evergreen mat-forming, wooly, gray leaves.

Sisyrinchium striatum. One of the joys of summer. The sword-shaped leaves and upright flower stems contribute to the upright, spiky display, and creamy yellow flowers appear in midsummer.

Rosa "Little White Pet." This patio rose also makes good ground-cover, if left alone. The white pompon flowers are produced from middle to late summer.

Osteospermum jucundum (African daisy). White daisy-like flowers cover this plant from early summer to fall, an ideal way of extending the flowering season in a small border.

WEST-FACING CORNER BED

This aspect means that the bed will not be in full sun until the afternoon. The sun will have reached its hottest by this time, so the area will warm up very quickly, making it a good choice for plants that require a sheltered site. Here, you can grow garden plants that require little maintenance, and which may not grow in other parts of the garden.

A predominantly pink scheme has been chosen, which is a good color for a west-facing border, and it will be highly scented in the early to middle part of the summer.

The Plants

3 *Agapanthus* "Loch Hope,"
5½ inch pots or larger

Artemisia "Powis Castle," 7½ inch pot

Itea ilicifolia, 7½ inch pot or larger

Jasminum officinale,
7½ inch pot or larger

3 *Rosa* "President de Seze,"
7½ inch pots or bare-rooted

2 *Salvia officinalis,* 6½ inch or
5½ inch pots

3 *Sedum spectabile,* 3½ inch or
5½ inch pots

Solanum crispum "Glasnevin's Variety,"
7½ inch pot or larger

Tools and Materials

Garden trowel • Spade
• Galvanized wire • Screw eyes

QUICK TIPS

HEATHER ANGEL

Agapanthus "Loch Hope"

Flowering season: early summer to early fall.

Soil: any good garden soil. Improve the soil each spring with well-rotted organic matter.

Care: these roses do not need pruning, but any dead wood should be removed in early spring. Cut the artemisia down hard in mid-spring, and also the sage if it has become poor and leggy in the winter. The climbers should be tied into wires on the wall or fence. Agapanthus is an excellent subject for a container, where it flowers better because its space is restricted. It must be brought into frost-free conditions to overwinter, in very cold areas.

Planting Plan

STEP ONE
Main Structural Planting

Solanum crispum "Glasnevin's Variety" (Climbing potato). The rich blue flowers of this climber, carried over a long period in midsummer, are a good companion for a variety of color schemes.

Itea ilicifolia (Sweetspire). This evergreen needs a protected site, and its loose habit means it is best grown against a wall or fence. The hanging flowers are sweetly scented and appear in late summer.

Rosa "President de Seze." The Gallica rose is probably the oldest of all garden roses, having been grown by the Greeks and Romans. Although only flowering once in early to midsummer, this Gallica rose provides a magnificent display, not to be missed. Attractive buds open to a full flower with a subtle mix of purple, violet, brown, and gray, with a sweet scent. Here, the artemisia, sage, and rose provide a perfect silver and pink combination.

Jasminum officinale (Jasmine). This summer-flowering jasmine is quite accommodating, and will even grow on a shady wall. Sweetly scented, it is an essential ingredient for a pretty country garden border.

In-fill Planting

Artemisia "Powis Castle." A stately plant, which always draws attention in the summer garden and has many uses in planting design. The gray foliage tones down any bright colors and helps to link shades which might otherwise be incompatible. It is a good choice in a traditional border, combining well with old roses and herbaceous plants.

GRAHAM A. PAVEY

Salvia officinalis (Sage). Matte, gray-green, evergreen leaves and a good shape combine to create a border plant of some distinction. It is the perfect foil for old roses and other country garden plants. Its understated presence does not interfere with the flowering of neighbors.

GRAHAM A. PAVEY

Agapanthus "Loch Hope." One of the most spectacular of all late-summer-flowering plants. Its blue flowers, growing in a candelabra style on the end of a long sturdy stem, are unforgettable, and will contrast with the pinks of the scheme to change the overall character. In early summer, its straplike leaves will provide a contrast in shape and texture. Later in the season, the emphasis will shift to the agapanthus and sedum combination, which will take up the baton for the end of the summer.

HEATHER ANGEL

Sedum spectabile (Showy stonecrop). Gray leaves in early summer combine well with the grays and pinks of the arrangement. The pink flowers, much loved by butterflies, flower with the agapanthus in late summer to continue the flowering season.

GARDEN MATTERS

69

NORTH-FACING CORNER BED

This is the shadiest of all the corner beds, but it is open to the sky and should not, therefore, be regarded as in full shade. Many plants prefer this aspect to a south-facing one, so the choice is not too limiting. Generally, colorful plants are not happy in shade, so the best approach is to create a scheme relying on shape and subdued colors. This scheme uses shades of green, some white, a little yellow, and one bold splash of red in the leaves of the heuchera.

The Plants

2 *Alchemilla mollis*, 3½ inch or
5½ inch pots

2 *Bergenia cordifolia*, 3½ inch or
5½ inch pots

Elaeagnus x *ebbingei* "Limelight,"
7½ inch pot

4 *Epimedium* x *versicolor* "Neo-Sulphureum,"
3½ inch or 5½ inch pots

3 *Heuchera* "Purple Palace," 3½ inch or
5½ inch pots

2 *Hydrangea petiolaris*, 7½ inch pots

Iris pallida "Variegata," 3½ inch or
5½ inch pot

2 *Rosa* "Iceberg," 7½ inch pots
or bare-rooted

Tools

Garden trowel • Spade

QUICK TIPS

GRAHAM A. PAVEY

Rosa "Iceberg"

Flowering season: the flowers are less important in this arrangement than in others, but there will be blooming from spring into midsummer.

Soil: any good garden soil. Improve the soil each spring with well-rotted organic matter.

Care: remove any dead wood from the roses in early spring and any dead material, such as leaves, from the perennials, as necessary. The climbing hydrangea is renowned for looking very sickly for three or four years after planting. This is nothing to worry about because the plant is concentrating on creating a sound root system, after which, it will quickly cover the wall or fence.

Planting Plan

Main Structural Planting

Hydrangea petiolaris (Climbing hydrangea). This spectacular plant will grow in quite deep shade, and has the added advantage of being self-clinging. Although not evergreen, its woody trunk and branches, with shaggy bark, make a solid structure in the winter.

Elaeagnus x *ebbingei* "Limelight." This reliable fast-growing evergreen brightens the garden at any time of year with its subtle silver-gold variegated leaves.

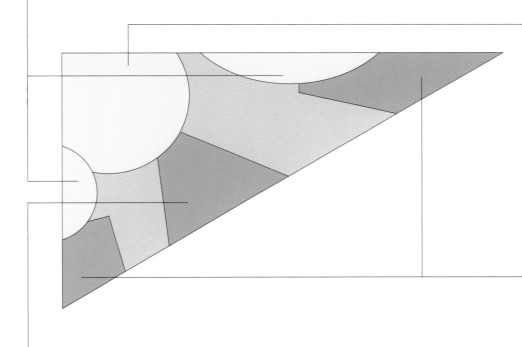

Epimedium x *versicolor* "Neo-Sulphureum" (Motherwort). Epimediums make excellent evergreen ground-cover plants for shady areas, especially in the woods. The pale yellow flowers appear in early spring, but are often hidden under the foliage. The top foliage can be cut away to reveal them, if desired.

Heuchera "Palace Purple." There are many varieties of this evergreen plant, but this is probably the best and most commonly grown. It has larger leaves than other varieties, and the purple leaves can be used either as a contrast to yellows or a companion for reds and pinks.

In-fill Planting

Rosa "Iceberg." Many roses are very useful shrubs for a mixed planting scheme, and "Iceberg" is no exception. Flowering for most of the summer, the small leaves and white flowers of *Rosa* "Iceberg" make a startling combination, and will work well in either sun or shade.

GRAHAM A. PAVEY

Iris pallida "Variegata." This attractive variegated iris adds a dramatic effect to the overall scheme, contrasting with the feathery foliage of the lady's mantle and the fern. The sword-shaped leaves of irises are a good way of adding interest to an otherwise "flat" planting scheme.

GRAHAM A. PAVEY

Alchemilla mollis (Lady's mantle). Growing in sun or shade, the lime-green, rounded, crinkly-edged foliage of this plant has no equal.

GRAHAM A. PAVEY

Bergenia cordifolia (Heartleaf bergenia). Bergenias are the perfect companion for many plants. Here, they combine well with *Heuchera* "Palace Purple," making a composition which works throughout the year. In small groups dotted around the garden, they help to tie a scheme together, although *en masse* bergenias can look untidy.

GRAHAM A. PAVEY

EAST-FACING LONG BORDER

These long borders are designed for medium-to-large gardens. For longer borders, duplicate along the whole length to make sure the border is a balanced success. This east-facing border will look its best early in the day when the yellows and blues will be lit up by the sun. A good position for it would be close to where breakfast is served, so it can be viewed either from a seating area in the garden or an appropriate window.

The Plants

Aucuba japonica "Variegata,"
7½ inch pot

2 *Buxus sempervirens* "Elegantissima,"
7½ inch pots

Clematis macropetala, 6½ inch or
7½ inch pot

10 *Delphinium* "Galahad," 3½ inch or
5½ inche pots

Euonymus fortunei "Silver Queen,"
6½ inch or 7½ inch pot

5 *Geranium* x *riversleaianum* "Russell
Prichard," 5½ inch or 6½ inch pots

5 *Hosta sieboldiana* "Frances Williams,"
5½ inch or 6½ inch pots

5 *Iris germanica,* 3½ inch or
5½ inch pots

2 *Mahonia japonica,* 7½ inch pots

2 *Rosa* "Graham Thomas" (Registered
name: Ausmas), 7½ inch pots
or bare-rooted

2 *Parthenocissus tricuspidata* "Veitchii,"
7½ inch pots

Philadelphus "Sybille," 7½ inch pot

2 *Pleioblastus viridistriatus,* 7½ inch pots
or larger

3 *Thalictrum aquilegiifolium,* 3½ inch or
5½ inch pots

3 *Viburnum opulus* "Compactum,"
6½ inche or 7½ inch pots

Tools

Garden trowel • Spade

QUICK TIPS

Flowering season: there are odd splashes of color throughout the year, but the main flowering season will be in late spring to midsummer. A combination of leaf shapes, shades of green, and different textures will maintain interest for a longer period than using flower color alone.

Soil: any good garden soil. Improve the soil each spring with well-rotted organic matter.

Care: Stake the delphiniums with strong canes in spring. Cut any dead wood out of the roses in early spring.

Viburnum opulus

Planting Plan

STEP ONE

Main Structural Planting

Mahonia japonica. This architectural plant looks good against a plain background where the foliage can stand out. Here, its evergreen foliage contributes to the structure of the arrangement. Scented flowers will appear in midwinter, and some may be out at Christmas.

GRAHAM A. PAVEY

Buxus sempervirens "Elegantissima" (Variegated boxwood). Boxwood is an excellent structural plant for use in either a formal setting or an informal garden style. The plain green plant is a large-growing shrub, eventually turning into a small tree, and needs constant attention. This variegated form is much better behaved and needs less effort.

GARDEN MATTERS

Philadelphus "Sybille" (Mock orange). Spectacular bell-shaped flowers, cascading down arching branches, combine with a sweet orange scent to make this plant one of the most popular for midsummer flowering.

GRAHAM A. PAVEY

Main Structural Planting
❧

Aucuba japonica "Variegata" (Japanese laurel). This is a truly excellent plant, growing in any conditions, including very deep shade. In spring, its golden foliage seems to glow when other plants are looking tired after the winter months.

GRAHAM A. PAVEY

Euonymus fortunei "Silver Queen." There are a large number of different varieties of the winter creeper – all of them easy, reliable evergreens. They can all be clipped like a hedge, and many will even climb a wall if grown against one.

GRAHAM A. PAVEY

Viburnum opulus "Compactum". This cranberry bush is a much better plant than its larger cousin. Its deciduous foliage comes right down to the ground, smothering any weeds, and the feathery foliage is an ideal companion for more solid leaves. Its white flowers appear in early summer.

GARDEN MATTERS

Pleioblastus viridistriatus. This bright yellow bamboo grows only to about 4 feet high, and unlike some other bamboos, it is quite well behaved. Here, its upright growth contrasts with the architectural shape of its neighbors.

GARDEN MATTERS

In-fill Planting

Parthenocissus tricuspidata "Veitchii" (Boston ivy). Related to the Virginia creeper, this is a much better plant. It will quickly grow over a wall or fence, where the Virginia creeper would rather scramble along the ground.

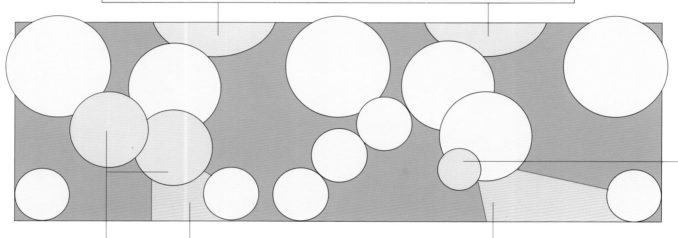

Rosa "Graham Thomas." In recent years, David Austin Roses have developed a collection of old-fashioned roses, with all the disease resistance of modern strains, which they call their "English Roses." This yellow shrub rose is one of the best of this collection, and has one of the longest flowering seasons. It is an excellent companion for variegated laurel. The color combinations are subtle and refined.

Geranium x *riversleaianum* "Russell Prichard." This hardy geranium is a little gem. It flowers from late spring to the first frosts without any particular attention. Its bright pink flowers are of a shade which combines well with a range of yellows, which is why it has been selected here.

Clematis macropetala. This small clematis flowers in early to late spring with rich blue nodding flowers. It is a good subject for a container. In the wild, clematis grows up through other plants, and here it has been used in a similar fashion, allowed to trail across the soil and grow up through plants naturally.

In-fill Planting

Iris germanica. No scheme is complete without sword- or spiky-shaped leaves, and this is easily added by using a variety of iris. *Iris germanica* is the most commonly grown bearded iris, and comes in a wide range of colors. Many are also scented. Any color would be suitable here.

GARDEN MATTERS

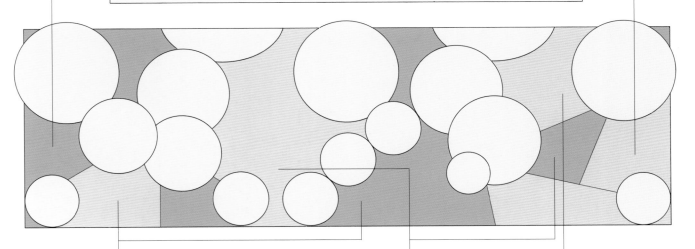

Hosta sieboldiana "Frances Williams." Hostas prefer a moist, shady site, but many will grow in drier conditions, and some can stand a degree of sun. The toughest are the *sieboldiana* varieties, of which this is one. The yellow variegated leaves are a good companion for more finely divided leaves.

GARDEN MATTERS

Delphinium "Galahad." No garden is complete without a grouping of delphiniums. Their spectacular display in midsummer gives impact to a border and provides an upright shape that contrasts with other plants.

GARDEN MATTERS

Thalictrum aquilegiifolium (Meadow rue). This stately plant has finely divided leaves and pink cottony flowers, all of which combine well with other plants.

GRAHAM A. PAVEY

SOUTH-FACING LONG BORDER

Being in the sun for most of the day, this border offers hot, dry conditions that are much loved by many of the more floriferous plants. Here, shape and texture have been maintained, but there is more emphasis on the flowering plants.

The Plants

Alchemilla mollis, 3½ inch or 5½ inch pot

Artemisia "Powis Castle," 5½ inch or 6½ inch pot

2 *Artemisia* "Silver Queen," 3½ inch or 5½ inch pots

4 *Bergenia cordifolia,* 3½ inch or 5½ inch pots

Carpentaria californica, 7½ inch pot or larger

2 *Ceanothus thyrsiflorus,* 7½ inch pots

6 *Delphinium* "Black Knight," 3½ inch or 5½ inch pots

Fremontodendron californicum, 7½ inch pot

Geranium psilostemon, 3½ inch or 5½ inch pot

2 *Lavandula angustifolia,* 5½ inch or 6½ inch pots

3 *Nepeta mussinii,* 3½ inch or 5½ inch pots

2 *Osteospermum* "Buttermilk," 3½ inch or 5½ inch pots

Phormium tenax purpureum, 7½ inch pot

2 *Rosmarinus officinalis,* 7½ inch pots

3 *Rosa* "Margaret Merril," 7½ inch pots or bare-rooted

2 *Salvia officinalis* "Purpurascens," 6½ inch or 7½ inch pots

2 *Sedum spectabile,* 3½ inch or 5½ inch pots

Taxus baccata "Fastigiata," 7½ inch pot

Vitis vinifera "Brandt," 7½ inch pot

Tools

Garden trowel • Spade • Galvanized wire • Screw eyes

GRAHAM A. PAVEY

Bergenia cordifolia

Flowering season: the main flowering season will be in late spring and early summer, although there will be color throughout the summer.

Soil: any good garden soil. Improve drainage by adding sharp sand at planting time, and incorporate well-rotted manure or compost around the roses in early spring.

Care: it is important to cut *Artemisia* "Powis Castle" to within a few inches of the ground in mid-spring to prevent it from becoming leggy. The lavender should be trimmed over after flowering, and again in spring. If the sage looks untidy and leggy in the spring, then cut it hard back to encourage regrowth from the base. Remove any dead wood from the roses in early spring.

During the summer season, dead head the roses and trim over the nepeta to insure a continuity of bloom. Stake the delphiniums with sturdy canes, and tie the climbers into the wires, as necessary.

Planting Plan

STEP ONE
Main Structural Planting

Ceanothus thyrsiflorus (California lilac). The brilliant display of blue flowers always makes this plant the center of attention in late spring, when it is at its best.

GRAHAM A. PAVEY

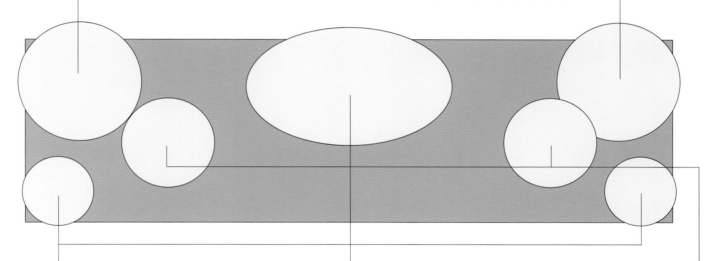

Lavandula angustifolia (Lavender). The common lavender flowers for a longer period than many of the hybrids, and the pale lilac flowers provide better, more subtle, support for the plant's neighbors.

GRAHAM A. PAVEY

Carpentaria californica. This evergreen shrub, festooned in white saucer-shaped flowers in midsummer, is the central feature of the border. It is certainly not a shy plant, and it will quickly establish itself.

GRAHAM A. PAVEY

Rosmarinus officinalis (Rosemary). Of all the ornamental herbs, this is the queen. Its upright spreading growth is unique. It combines well in a country garden or in a warm, sunny border, where its blue flowers and aromatic gray foliage provide solid support.

GRAHAM A. PAVEY

STEP TWO
In-fill Planting

Artemisia "Powis Castle." The silver-gray feathery leaves of this plant make it the perfect choice for any sunny border.

GRAHAM A. PAVEY

Phormium tenax purpureum (New Zealand flax). The bold straplike leaves make this a plant for impact. The purple foliage will combine and complement the blues, whites, and pink of its neighbors.

GRAHAM A. PAVEY

Rosa "Margaret Merril." For scent, this rose has no equal. The flesh-colored blooms are held over glossy, healthy leaves all summer long.

R. HARKNESS & CO.

Salvia officinalis "Purpurascens" (Purple sage). There are a number of ornamental sages available, and each one is useful for combining with other gray-leaf plants, herbaceous perennials, and roses.

GRAHAM A. PAVEY

Taxus baccata "Fastigiata" (Irish yew). Upright, or fastigiate, conifers are a useful addition to a border when different shapes are needed. All forms of the common yew are very tough plants, equally at home in deep shade and in full sun.

GRAHAM A. PAVEY

STEP THREE
In-fill Planting

Vitis vinifera "Brandt." This ornamental grapevine is an extremely useful garden plant. It will grow anywhere, including dry shade – although in these conditions, the grapes can be forgotten. The foliage is attractively divided and colors up well in the fall.

Geranium psilostemon. This stately plant is the tallest of the hardy geraniums. The bright magenta flowers are held above self-supporting stems for a long period in midsummer. Here, the geranium works well with the light, feathery silver foliage of *Artemisia* "Powis Castle."

Fremontodendron californicum (Fremontia). Large yellow flowers, carried on this evergreen plant throughout the summer, make this one of the special sights of summer. The combination of this plant with ceanothus is quite breathtaking.
Warning: the dusty down on the leaves can irritate the skin, so wash your hands after handling it, or wear gloves.

Bergenia cordifolia (Heartleaf bergenia) The large, leathery leaves of the bergenia are used as a solid contrast to the more feathery foliage in the scheme – here, the foliage of *Geranium psilostemon.* The bright pink flowers are a welcome splash of color at the end of the winter.

Sedum spectabile (Showy stonecrop). Late summer would not be the same without the flat heads of the sedum. These bright pink flowers attract butterflies and bees in great numbers.

Delphinium "Black Knight." The tall stems of the delphinium will pick up the fastigiate shape of the Irish yew, and contrast with the other shapes in the plan.

GRAHAM A. PAVEY

Artemisia ludoviciana "Silver Queen." This herbaceous artemisia is more open than the shrubby "Powis Castle," and dies down in the winter. The silvery foliage is finely cut, making a spectacular display.

HEATHER ANGEL

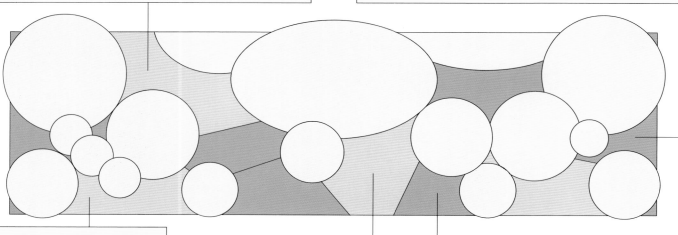

Alchemilla mollis (Lady's mantle). Every garden should incorporate this plant somewhere. The lime-green flowers combine well with any color scheme and especially with roses and herbaceous plants. It will seed itself around freely, and the seedlings seem to thrive wherever they appear. Here, the catnip and lady's mantle look good planted as close neighbors. The contrasting shapes complement each other to create an attractive combination.

GRAHAM A. PAVEY

Nepeta mussinii (Catnip). Pale lilac flowers are held on long stems throughout the summer months, and make a good companion for feathery foliage plants like lady's mantle.

GRAHAM A. PAVEY

Osteospermum "Stardust" (African daisy). Mauve flowers, produced from spring to fall, keep interest in the border throughout much of the year.

GRAHAM A. PAVEY

WEST-FACING LONG BORDER

Warming up later in the day, the west-facing border offers one of the best sheltered spots in the garden – a place where plants that would not survive in other parts of the garden can be grown.

Some of the best effects in a garden can be created by using only a small number of different varieties. It may take a little courage to do, but the final show can be stunning.

The Plants

2 *Choisya ternata*, 7½ inch pots or larger

9 *Geranium* x *riversleaianum* "Mavis Simpson," 5½ inch or 6½ inch pots

2 *Lavandula angustifolia* "Munstead," 6½ inch or 7½ inch pots

Rosa "Nevada," 7½ inch pot or bare-rooted

Rosa "Scarlet Fire," 7½ inch pot or bare-rooted

12 *Stachys byzantina* "Silver Carpet," 3½ inch or 5½ inch pots

6 *Yucca recurvifolia*, 7½ inch pots or larger

Tools

Garden trowel • Spade

QUICK TIPS

GRAHAM A. PAVEY

Rosa "Nevada".

Flowering season: the main flowering season is in middle to late summer, a time when many gardens begin to look exhausted as they await the late summer-flowering surge.

Soil: any good garden soil.

Care: the main task is to trim over the lavender after it has flowered, and again in early or mid-spring. This will help to maintain the overall shape of the plant. Remove any flower heads that appear on the lamb's-ears immediately. Remove any dead wood from the roses in early spring.

Planting Plan

STEP ONE
Main Structural Planting

Rosa "Scarlet Fire." This large shrub rose has one spectacular display of brilliant red flowers in midsummer, followed by bright red rose hips.

Rosa "Nevada." This large shrub rose is festooned in early and late summer with large, white, saucer-shaped flowers, making it the perfect choice for a large border. The size and color of its flowers make it a good companion for *Rosa* "Scarlet Fire."

Choisya ternata (Mexican orange blossom). One of the best evergreens available, it will grow in sun or shade. It has a "skirt" that comes down to the ground, smothering any weeds. The flowers in late spring have an orange scent, and the leaves are aromatic when crushed.

Yucca recurvifolia. Spiky leaves add impact to a border. Here, a yucca has been selected. This evergreen plant will develop tall spires of bell-shaped white flowers in late summer, when the border will be at its best.

Infill Planting

Lavandula angustifolia "Munstead." This plant has dark violet-blue flowers – much darker than the ordinary lavender. It is also lower-growing and more compact.

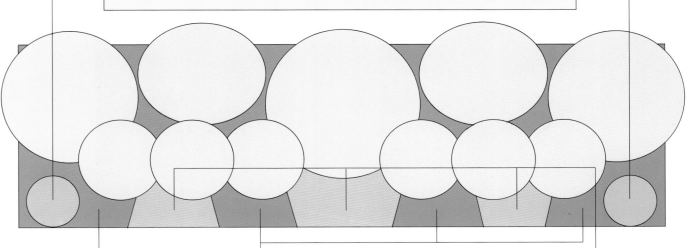

Stachys byzantina "Silver Carpet" (Lamb's-ears). The flowers of this plant are not particularly attractive and distort the overall shape. The variety "Silver Carpet" is a nonflowering variety. The combination of lavender, yucca, and lamb's-ears makes a good display on its own, without the addition of other plants.

Geranium x *riversleaianum* "Mavis Simpson." Flowers for most of the summer, combined with pale gray-green foliage, make this a much-treasured hardy geranium. The geranium will grow through the lamb's-ears in time, making it appear that the latter has pink flowers.

NORTH-FACING LONG BORDER

This aspect is satisfying to plant up. Although lacking in bright color, this can be more than compensated for by using the best foliage and scents.

Cool colors, such as blues, mauves, pale pinks, and cream, are the best choices for a shady site; hot colors, such as reds and oranges, are much better in full sun.

The Plants

Amelanchier lamarkii, 7½ inch pot or larger

2 *Clematis* "Perle D'Azur," 7½ inch pots

2 *Fatsia japonica,* 7½ inch pots or larger

9 *Hosta tokudama,* 3½ inch or 5½ inch pots

9 *Hosta undulata* var. *undulata,* 3½ inch or 5½ inch pots

2 *Jasminum humile revolutum,* 7½ inch pots

2 *Lonicera pileata,* 7½ inch pots

10 *Rodgersia pinnata* "Superba," 5½ inch or 6½ inch pots

Tools

Garden trowel • Spade

QUICK TIPS

Hostas and rodgersias

Flowering season: this is less important with this scheme than with others, but the main flourish is in early summer to midsummer.

Soil: any good garden soil. Add well-rotted manure or compost in early spring.

Care: slug pellets around the hostas will reduce any possible damage by snails and slugs. It is essential to plant the clematis roots away from the center of the host plant, so the competition between the two plants is minimal.

Planting Plan

Main Structural Planting

Jasminum humile revolutum (Shrubby jasmine). Mention jasmine and most people think of a climber with scented white flowers. There are, however, a number of medium-to-large shrubby jasmines, mainly with yellow flowers. This one flowers from late summer to fall.

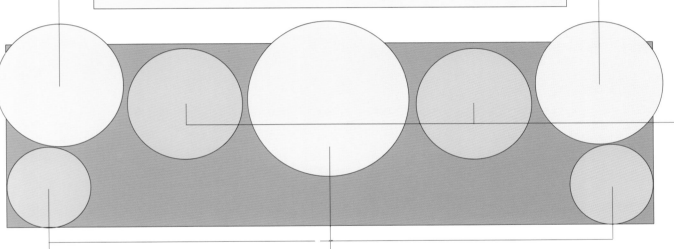

Lonicera pileata. This close relative of honeysuckle is an excellent ground-covering plant. Its outward and upward pointing branches offer an unusual shrub shape to the overall border.

Amelanchier lamarkii (Service berry). This has to be one of the choicest plants for any garden. It will grow in sun or shade, starting the season off in mid-spring with sweet-scented white blossom, and finishing the season with a brilliant foliage display in the fall.

Fatsia japonica (Japanese aralia). This large-leaf evergreen looks more like an atrium plant than a garden plant, with large, glossy leaves held in palmate clusters. It has the advantage of being happy in quite deep shade, including the shade cast by a large tree.

STEP TWO
In-fill Planting

Clematis "Perle D'Azur." A good way of growing clematis is through and over other shrubs. Here, a large-flowered hybrid clematis grows through the shrubby jasmine. The blue flowers of the clematis contrast with the yellow flowers of the jasmine in a particularly successful combination.

GARDEN MATTERS

Rodgersia pinnata "Superba". This plant is generally regarded as a bog-garden plant, where it will quickly become established at the expense of other plants. In an ordinary border, as long as it has some shade and the root run does not become too dry, it is perfectly happy and will increase in size very slowly.

GRAHAM A. PAVEY

Hosta "Tokudama." This blue-leaf hosta is an ideal companion for the previous two plants, contrasting in both shape and color.

DIANA GRENFELL

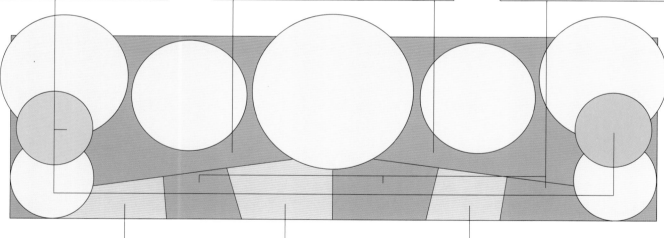

Hosta undulata var. *undulata*. This is one of the finest of the small-leaf variegated hostas. It is unusual because the variegation is in the form of a white line down the center of each leaf. The lilac flowers in late summer are a bonus. Cool colors are ideal in a shady situation, and this combination of hostas and rodgersias is perfect.

GRAHAM A. PAVEY

BOG GARDEN

*A*reas of garden where the soil is constantly damp are a fairly common occurrence close to a natural pond, lake, or spring. Many plants have evolved to cope with these conditions, and with careful plant selection, the area can become an important garden feature. If a natural area does not exist, it is possible to create an artificial one, either close to a man-made pond or, perhaps, in a border among other plants.

The Plants

Acer palmatum var. *dissectum*,
7½ inch pot

8 *Astilbe* x *arendsii* "Venus," 5½ inch or
6½ inch pots

5 *Crocosmia* "Lucifer," 3½ inch or
5½ inch pots

3 *Houttuynia cordata* "Chameleon,"
3½ inch or 5½ inch pots

5 *Iris pseudoacorus* "Variegata,"
3½ inch or 5½ inch pots

4 *Lobelia* "Queen Victoria,"
3½ inch or 5½ inch pots

Phormium tenax,
6½ inch or 7½ inch pot

7 *Polygonum bistorta* "Superbum,"
3½ inch or 5½ inch pots

1 *Rheum palmatum*, 6½ inch or
8½ inch pots

7 *Rodgersia aesculifolia*, 3½ inch
or 5½ inch pots

4 *Zantedeschia aethiopia*, 6½ inch
or 7½ inch pots

Tools

Spade • Garden trowel

QUICK TIPS

GRAHAM A. PAVEY

Astilbe x *arendsii*

Flowering season: summer. The bold leaf shapes of the rhubarb and tne white-flowered rodgersia make a dramatic combination. The hot colors in this border combine to catch the eye from every part of the garden.

Soil: any good garden soil, which is damp all year-round, but not under water. If these conditions do not exist naturally, excavate the soil to a spade's depth and introduce a piece of rubber or plastic, perforated in several places to allow excess water to escape. Make sure a hollow is created by mounding the soil around the edge, under the plastic.

Care: Provided the soil is constantly moist, these plants will grow in full sun. Apart from cutting down dead foliage in the fall, there should be no maintenance needed.

Planting Plan

Main Structural Planting

Acer palmatum var. *dissectum* (Japanese maple). Often difficult to place, this low-growing shrub prefers a sheltered site and acid soil. The damp conditions in a bog garden simulate acid soil, and the moisture insures that any drying by the wind, so often the enemy of these plants, is minimized.

Zantedeschia aethiopica (Calla lily). The creamy white, funnel-shaped flower spike of this plant is like the best porcelain, and the plant is a great favorite. Try growing it in a container.

GRAHAM A. PAVEY

Pond

11 ft

16 ft

8 ft

Phormium tenax (New Zealand flax). Regarded as an exotic shrub, this plant is often thought to be a slightly tender sun-lover, but in fact, it grows in marshy ground in its native home and is perfect for the water's edge.

GRAHAM A. PAVEY

Crocosmia "Lucifer" (Montbretia). The brilliant color of this montbretia combines well with the hot colors in this scheme. Normally found in the flower border, this versatile plant is happy in a range of conditions, including those of a bog garden.

GRAHAM A. PAVEY

Polygonum bistorta "Superbum" (Knotweed). Growing anywhere, these low evergreen plants are useful for ground-cover. The pink bulrush-shaped flower heads are held over a long period in midsummer.

Rheum palmatum (Ornamental rhubarb). This statuesque plant resembles rhubarb only in the size and appearance of its leaves. It needs a moist soil, but can cope with drier conditions when established.

Pond

Astilbe x *arendsii* "Venus" (False spirea). Feathery foliage and pink flowers with the texture of cotton make this a highly desirable garden plant. It is often planted in the mixed border, where it dies out through lack of moisture.

Houttuynia cordata "Chameleon." This ground-cover plant is at much as home in the flower border as it is in the bog garden. The multicolored evergreen leaves are really stunning.

Iris pseudoacorus "Variegata." As has been said before in this book, the spiky shape is an important ingredient in any planting plan, and the bog garden is no exception. Iris is always a good choice. It will also grow in an ordinary mixed border and in shallow water.

GRAHAM A. PAVEY

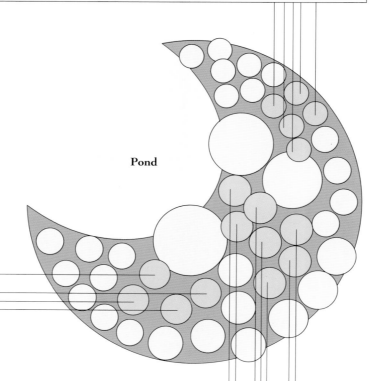

Pond

Lobelia "Queen Victoria." For brilliance of color, no plant can outperform this tall-growing lobelia. It is short-lived, and may need replacing every two or three years.

GRAHAM A. PAVEY

Rodgersia aesculifolia. The large leaves of this plant resemble those of the horse chestnut, and they make an excellent contrast for many other bog-garden plants. Although happier in a moist soil, it will grow in a shady border where the soil does not become too warm.

GARDEN MATTERS

WOODLAND BED

*W*here there has been a lot of decaying matter in the soil over a number of years, usually in woodland, the pH of the soil drops and becomes more acid. Many plants have become dependent on this type of soil, notably rhododendrons and most heathers, and cannot grow in alkaline conditions. This border has been designed to make full use of these acid-loving plants. The best site for it would be on the edge of woodland or in a clearing in partial shade, where it can get some sun, but not too much.

The Plants

Acer griseum in 8½ inch pot or larger

20 *Hyacinthoides nonscripta* bulbs

Kalmia latifolia, 7½ inch pot

3 *Lilium martagon,* 3½ inch or 5½ inch pots, or 3 bulbs

Magnolia x *soulangeana* "Brizoni," 7½ inch pot or larger

2 *Rhododendron* "Cecile," 7½ inch pots

3 *Rhododendron* "Susan," 7½ inch pots

3 *Skimmia laureola,* 7½ inch pots

Tools

Spade • Garden trowel

QUICK TIPS

Magnolia soulangeana and *Rhododendron*

Flowering season: spring and early summer. Combining magnolias and azaleas is the perfect way to make sure that spring remains an unforgettable time of the year. The deep blue of the English bluebell and the red of this rhododendron make a dramatic combination.

Care: the soil must have plenty of organic matter and peat, so it is rich and acid. The plants do best in partial shade with some sunshine for part of the day.

Rhododendron "Susan" with English bluebells

Planting Plan

Main Structural Planting

Magnolia x *soulangeana* "Brizoni." A magnolia in full flower is one of those unforgettable sights of spring. Although not evergreen, the bare tree in winter has a fine architectural shape, which contributes to the structure of the garden.

GARDEN MATTERS

Rhododendron "Cecile" (Azalea). The spring-flowering azaleas are a magnificent introduction to spring in any garden lucky enough to have an acid soil. They are good companions for magnolias.

GARDEN MATTERS

Acer griseum (Paper-bark maple). Many trees are grown for their bark, but nothing is quite like this unusual maple. The peeling bark is like flaked chocolate, and it is always a conversation point. It will grow in any soil.

GRAHAM A. PAVEY

Rhododendron "Susan." This evergreen rhododendron, with its large clusters of red flowers, will always dominate a border, and it has been used here for impact.

GARDEN MATTERS

Kalmia latifolia (Mountain laurel). The early summer-flowering of this evergreen shrub will help to extend the flowering season of the border.

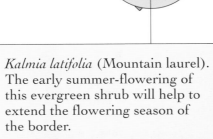

GRAHAM A. PAVEY

Skimmia laureola. In order to get red berries on a skimmia, a male plant must be planted close to a female. This variety is male, so there will be no berries, but the scent is better than that of the female, and will be most welcome in early spring.

GARDEN MATTERS

Lilium martagon (Martagon lily). This unusual bulbous plant will seed itself throughout the border, raising its head above the foliage where it is least expected without becoming a nuisance.

GRAHAM A. PAVEY

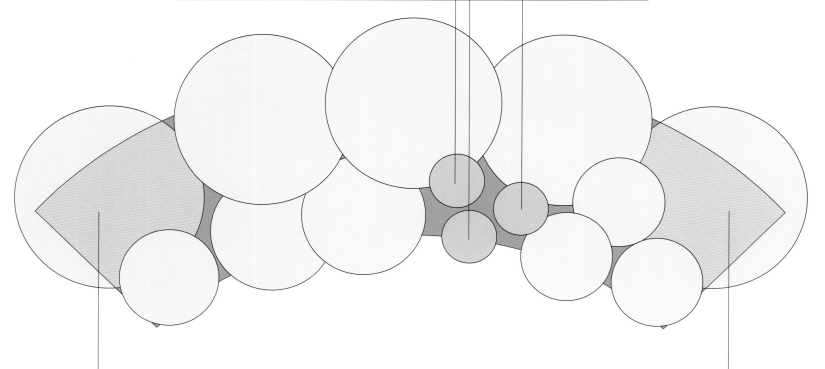

Hyacinthoides nonscripta (English bluebells). Also called wild hyacinths, these are the beautiful flowers of old English bluebell woods. They are the perfect companion for rhododendrons and azaleas.

GARDEN MATTERS

HERB
GARDENS

*Simple projects using herbs
to their full potential as
ornamental plants for the garden*

INTRODUCTION

P arsley, sage, rosemary, and thyme are just some of the aromatic herbs, with their culinary, perfumery, or medicinal uses that have been cultivated through the centuries, from the earliest monastic and physic gardens to their more recent revival as easy-to-grow, ornamental plants. With careful selection, and a little imagination, herbs can be used to enhance our gardens and homes, as well as serving a practical purpose.

In this book, we explore ways of using herbs to their fullest potential. Plants like mugwort, horseradish, or horehound, which serve little useful purpose and can become serious pests in the garden, are not used. The herbs in this book are useful in the kitchen or for their scent, and as decorative and ornamental plants for the flower garden.

From the traditional herb wheel through to the more innovative herb cascade, the projects offer something for every gardener. There are larger projects, which can be incorporated into the overall design of a garden, and simple schemes designed to provide a quick and easy method of making herbs available to the kitchen.

GARDEN MATTERS

GARDEN MATTERS

MATERIALS AND TECHNIQUES

The Herbs

Many herbs are invasive colonizers, either by underground root systems or by seed. Several of the designs in this book show herbs grown in sections separated by brick or paving, a method which helps to contain the plants' roots. In some instances, especially with the mints, it may be necessary to plant the herb inside a bucket or container. This must be at least 12 inches deep, with the bottom removed. Plants which spread rapidly by seed, like golden feverfew, are best clipped when the flowers appear to stop them setting seed.

For most projects, the smallest plants will be suitable, but some plants, like rosemary and sage, unless for a special use, are better purchased as much larger specimens. Plants are usually sold by the size of the pot they are grown in, 3½ inches being the smallest. The recommended plant size is shown against the plant in each project.

Most of the herbs in this book can be used in the kitchen, bathroom, or medicine cabinet, while others are purely ornamental.

Angelica Candied angelica is used as a cake decoration. Angelica leaves are also good for adding to rhubarb instead of sugar.
Artemisia "Powis Castle" The beautiful silvery gray foliage of this plant is a perfect foil for green-leaved herbs. Its close relative, wormwood, can be used as a moth repellent.

Angelica
(*Angelica
archangelica*).

Basil This plant comes in many different varieties, with a wide range of leaf color and shape. It is a good accompaniment to meat, eggs, mushrooms, and tomatoes, and an integral part of Italian cooking, adding flavor to pasta and pizzas.

Bay (*Laurus nobilis*).

Bay Used in soups, stews, and stocks containing fish, meat, poultry, and game. The fresh leaves have a stronger flavor than the dried ones.

Bee balm (*Monarda didyma*).

Bee balm This showy herb is just as easily at home in a mixed flower border as in a herb garden. The leaves can be added sparingly to salads and are a good accompaniment to pork.

The flowers keep their fragrance and color when dried and are an important ingredient for potpourris.

*The first herbal was published in America in 1569 by Nicholas Monardes. Bee balm (*Monarda didyma*) commemorates him. The Native Americans, who introduced the settlers to many new herbs, used it to make a tea called Oswego.*

Chamomile (*Chamaemelum nobile*).

Chamomile Mainly used for cosmetics and medicines, it can also be used to make camomile tea, which is said to improve the appetite. Chamomile oil added to bath water will aid relaxation.
Caraway The seeds are used in pies, cookies, bread, and apple dishes, while the root can be cooked as a vegetable.

Catnip (*Nepeta racemosa*).

Catnip Catnip has some medicinal properties. It is much loved by cats who enjoy rolling in it.
Chervil One of the "fines herbes," much used in French cuisine, it has a delicate flavor with a touch of aniseed. Use leaves in salads, soups, sauces, vegetables, chicken, and fish dishes.

Chives (*Allium schoenoprasum*).

Chives Good in soups, fish, egg dishes, cream cheese, and with potatoes. It is also used in salads where the edible purple flowers can be used for decoration.
Coriander Two parts of this plant are of use. The leaves, called cilantro, can be used sparingly to garnish salads, curries, stews, and sauces, and the seeds, which have a different flavor, are used to flavor curries, rice, tomato, and avocado dishes.

Curry plant (*Helichrysum italicum*).

Curry plant Although the leaves have a strong scent, it is lost in cooking, but they can be added to rice and vegetables after cooking to introduce a mild curry flavor.

Fennel *(Foeniculum vulgare)*.

Fennel Fennel is good with fish, pork, veal, chicken, and young vegetables. In the garden, fennel attracts syrphid flies, voracious feeders of whitefly, so making a practical, as well as a culinary and ornamental, contribution.

Tarragon *(Artemisia dracunculus)*.

Tarragon This is a good accompaniment to many foods, including veal, poultry and game, seafood, egg dishes, vegetables, and tomatoes. Henry VIII is believed to have divorced Catherine of Aragon for her reckless use of the herb!

Tarragon is best planted in a bottomless flowerpot or bucket to help contain its invasive underground runners.

Golden feverfew *(Chrysanthemum parthenium)*.

Golden feverfew Used in medicine, mainly for treating migraines, this plant has no culinary use.

Roast-beef plant *(Iris foetidissima)*.

Roast-beef plant *(Iris foetidissima)* Grown as an ornamental plant, the spiky leaves and bright orange berries in fall add height and color to a border, even in quite deep shade.

Lady's mantle *(Alchemilla mollis)*.

Lady's mantle Used by herbalists to treat menstrual disorders, there are no culinary uses for this plant, but it is an attractive addition to the flower garden.

Golden oregano *(Origanum vulgare "Aureum")*.

Oregano, or wild marjoram, combines well with tomato, meat, and pizza dishes, and is the main ingredient of bouquet garni.

Moroccan mint *(Mentha spicata)*.

Apple mint *(Mentha suaveolens)*.

Spearmint *(Mentha spicata)*.

Mint There are many species of mint available to the gardener. It is good with lamb, veal, fish, potatoes, and peas, and in drinks and fruit punches. Mint has long been cultivated for its aromatic, culinary, and antiseptic qualities. Nearly all are invasive creeping plants, and are best planted in bottomless containers to curb their spreading underground roots.

Parsley (*Petrosalinium crispum*).

Parsley Excellent for use in soups and stews, and with lamb, parsley is also good with fish and in stuffing for poultry and game. Omelets and vegetables benefit from the addition of some parsley, and it is used as a garnish to many dishes.

Rosemary (*Rosmarinus officinalis*).

Rosemary Ideal for use with pork, lamb, and chicken, rosemary is also cultivated for its aromatic oils. Rosemary can be grown as a hedge, the clippings dried and used in the kitchen throughout the year.
Rue This bitter herb is cultivated for its decorative, glaucous leaves and is believed to have magical properties – particularly if obtained by theft.

GRAHAM A. PAVEY

LEFT: Golden sage (*Salvia officinalis* "Icterina").
RIGHT: Sage (*Salvia officinalis*).

Sage An excellent accompaniment for pork, goose, duck, and oily fish, sage has deliciously aromatic foliage and is widely cultivated for medicinal uses.
Sweet cicely The root can be cooked as a vegetable or eaten raw. The leaves have an aniseed flavor and can be added to salads, or chopped and added to soups and stews.
Soapwort or bouncing Bet This plant has no culinary uses, but is used medicinally to treat skin conditions.
Strawberry Strawberries are very ornamental plants, and any variety can be used to brighten up a herb garden. The fruit can be used in salads, desserts, or simply eaten on their own. A tea can be made from the leaves.

Thyme (*Thymus* "Doone Valley").

Thyme Thymes are good in soups, meat stews, stuffing for poultry, salads, and also combines well with fish and vegetables. They retain their fragrance well on drying, and are used in potpourris and herb pillows. In the Middle Ages, thyme was a symbol of courage, and high-ranking ladies embroidered sprigs onto the clothes of knights off to the Crusades.

Building Materials

Bricks come in a range of hardness, from very soft stock bricks to very hard engineering bricks. The softer the bricks, the more prone they are to attack by frost. Softer bricks have a more attractive texture and may be desirable from a design point of view. Frost-damaged bricks can also be a feature in themselves. If using soft bricks, buy some extra ones for use at a later date to replace any breakages. House bricks would a good choice, but there is a wide range of materials, from concrete pavers to granite setts. The key is to make sure they fit with your overall plan.

Use a level and brick hammer to make sure the bricks are laid flat.

Hardcore consists of any form of rubble, broken up with the brick hammer and squashed into place at the base of an excavation, ready for laying paving. Old bricks, concrete, stones, or any solid waste material could be used.
Lean mix is 6 parts builder's sand to 1 part cement, with a little water added to damp it down slightly and make it easy to use. This mixture will dry to a solid base. When pointing between the bricks, care should be taken to avoid soiling the brick face.
Concrete cement mix is 6 parts builder's sand to 1 part cement, mixed with water to form a cake-mix consistency. It is used for laying paving slabs.

Soils

Herbs are diverse in their soil requirements. Many are sun-lovers enjoying dry, impoverished conditions, but some, such as parsley, require better treatment.

The best approach is not to feed the soil, but to deal with the hungry plants individually. If you have a clay soil, it would be beneficial to break this up by digging in sharp sand to improve drainage, but do not go any deeper than a spade's depth because you may bring some undesirable subsoil to the surface.

For containers, **peat-based potting soil** has the advantage of being light, so is ideal in hanging baskets and containers that are intended to be moved around. The disadvantage is that it dries out very quickly. Because the extraction of peat moss and the damage to peat beds is environmentally unsound, seek out a manufacturer with a sound policy of obtaining peat from managed peat beds.

Peat-based potting soil.

Soil-based potting soil.

Moss.   CENTER: *Shredded forest bark.*   *Sharp sand.*

Alternative commercial soils, based on shredded forest bark, are viable alternatives, as is coir, or coconut fiber, although the extraction of this, too, is said to be having a detrimental effect on its native soil.

Soil-based potting soil is heavier, and is best used in containers which are permanently sited. It has the advantage of remaining moist longer.

Moss is used to line hanging baskets. It is easily obtainable from garden centers, or an alternative source is moss raked from the lawn, but you must make sure that no chemicals have been used to treat the grass.

Sharp sand should be dug into heavy, clay soils to break up the texture and improve drainage. Any clean sand could be used instead, but avoid yellow builder's sand because this can be very dirty and greasy.

Plant Care

Regular maintenance of plants will help keep their attractive appearance.

Watering herbs regularly is important, but many herbs from hot, dry countries have aromatic oils in their leaves and stems, which help to reduce water loss through evaporation, and enable the plant to cope with dry conditions more effectively. Many herbs need less watering than other plants and will tolerate neglect. There are some exceptions, and these are indicated in each project. The ability to cope with dry conditions makes many herbs perfect subjects for containers.

Watering should, ideally, be carried out first thing in the morning. Care should be taken to avoid splashing water on the leaves because this can cause them to scorch in the sun.

Regular maintenance of plants will help to keep their attractive appearance. Many herbs start off the growing season looking fresh and inviting, but by late summer become scruffy. This usually happens when they have set seed, so the first solution is to trim off any flower stems that appear, or deadhead regularly. This will help to keep the plant bushy and encourage new growth.

The drastic and final solution is to cut the plant down to the ground, which removes it until the next season; or, if it is grown in a container, remove it to a place out of sight.

Tools and equipment

Use a **garden trowel** for digging holes for planting small plants.

A **garden rake** should be used to prepare the soil surface once an area of soil has been dug over. The surface is raked, to create a fine tilth that is ready for planting, by dragging the rake backward and forward across the area.

You will need a **spade** for digging over beds and borders before planting, and for planting larger plant specimens.

A **wheelbarrow** is essential for moving soil and sand around when preparing a border. It is also useful for mixing sand and cement.

Crockery shards are needed for drainage in the bottom of containers. The best are broken bits of terra-cotta flowerpots, although broken tiles or medium-size stones collected from the garden would also suffice.

A **builder's line** is a very useful piece of equipment to insure the bricks are laid in a straight line. One can be made with strong cord and two wooden stakes.

Use a **level** to make sure that any bricks or paving are laid flat.

A **stake,** such as a short piece of wood, or metal, or a tent peg with line attached, is used as the center point for marking out a circle.

A **brick hammer** is needed throughout the projects for leveling bricks and paving.

A **bricklayer's trowel** is used for mixing and placing cement, and is essential for pointing between bricks or paving.

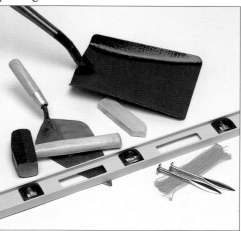

HERB CASCADE

This unusual way of growing herbs was discovered in an old Victorian gardening book. In addition to herbs, alpines and bedding plants can be grown in this way, and the effect can be quite stunning. *The ideal place for the herb cascade would be close to the kitchen door, or even in a sunroom, where the herbs could easily be harvested as required. It could also be used as part of a group of containers on a patio.*

Materials

Five terra-cotta flowerpots, one each of diameter 15½ inches; 13 inches; 10½ inches; 8 inches; and 6½ inches • Crockery shards • Peat-based potting soil

CARE

Although most of the plants in this scheme are perennials, they may need replacing each spring to keep the arrangement fresh. The parsley will need replacing each year.

The Plants

A. *3 alpine strawberry (Fragaria vesca "Semperflorens"), 3½ inch pots*

B. *3 thyme (Thymus serpyllum coccineus "Major"), 3½ inch pots*

C. *3 parsley (Petroselinum crispum), 3½ inch pots*

D. *2 chives (Allium schoenoprasum) 3½ inch pots*

E. *1 silver mint (Mentha longifolia), 3½ inch pots*

1. Starting with the largest pot, cover the base of the pot with a generous layer of shards to aid drainage.

2. Add peat-based or lightweight potting soil so the arrangement will not be too heavy to move.

3. Bring the soil up to a level where the second pot will sit comfortably with the base of its rim against the top of the first pot. Keep trying the pot out until the desired level is found.

4. Making sure that the second pot is firmly held in place against the back of the first pot, fill in with soil, firming and consolidating to insure a solid fit. The occasional tap against the pot will help to settle the soil.

5. Repeat the process with the other pots until the whole cascade is completed.

Planting Plan

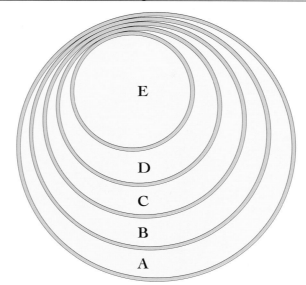

1. Starting on the bottom tier, carefully plant up each level. Tease out the roots of each plant before you plant it, so they will quickly start to grow into the new soil. Plant the 3 alpine strawberry plants in Pot A.
2. Next plant the 3 thymes in Pot B.
3. The 3 parsley plants should be planted in Pot C.
4. In Pot D, plant the 2 chives.
5. The cascade is topped with a silver mint planted in Pot E. The completed cascade will quickly mature if planted in the spring.

ALTERNATIVE PLANTING SCHEME

Pot A.
3 golden oregano (*Origanum vulgare* "Aureum"), 3½ inch pots

Pot B.
3 soapwort or bouncing Bet (*Saponaria ocymoides*), 3½ inch pots

Pot C.
2 chives (*Allium schoenoprasum*), 3½ inch pots

Pot D.
3 purple basil (*Ocimum basilicum* var. *purpurascens*), 3½ inch pots

Pot E.
1 rosemary (*Rosmarinus officinalis*), 5½ inch pot

HERB LADDER

*T*his traditional design is a very flexible way of growing herbs in a large area. The space between each "rung" provides a section where the more invasive plants can be restrained, and the bricks make it easy to access each plant. The scheme can be made larger by adding more "rungs," or adding a second ladder alongside the first. The perfect setting for a herb ladder in the garden would be beside a path or patio, perhaps forming an interlock between the hard surface and a flower border. As the plants mature, the sages and chamomile will grow over the brickwork and path, blurring and softening the hard edges.

By using the same brick in the ladder as that used in the construction of the house, you can create a "link" between the house and the garden.

The Plants

A. *6 chamomile (Chamaemelum nobile "Treneague"), 3½ inch pots*

B. *2 golden sage (Salvia officinalis "Icterina"), 6½ inch or 8½ inch pots*

C. *1 rue (Ruta graveolens "Jackman's Blue"), 3½ inch or 6½ inch pot*

D. *2 purple sage (Salvia officinalis "Purpurescens"), 6½ inch or 8½ inch pots*

E. *2 chives (Allium schoenoprasum), 3½ inch or 5½ inch pots*

F. *1 tarragon (Artemisia dracunculus), 5½ inch or 6½ inch pot*

G. *3 golden feverfew (Chrysanthemum parthenium "Aureum"), 3½ inch pots*

H. *1 curry plant (Helichrysum italicum), 3½ inch or 5½ inch pot*

I. *1 bronze fennel (Foeniculum vulgare "Purpureum"), 3½ inch or 5½ inch pot*

Materials

90 bricks • Lean mix (1 part cement to 6 parts builder's sand) • Builder's line • Level • Brick hammer • Spade • Bricklayer's trowel • Garden trowel

J. *2 lemon thyme (Thymus × citriodorus "Aureus"), 3½ inch pots*

K. *1 apple mint (Mentha suaveolens), 6½ inch or 8½ inch pot*

L. *1 basil (Ocimum basilicum), 3½ inch or 5½ inch pot*

M. *2 parsley (Petroselinum crispum), 3½ inch pots*

1. Start with the "uprights" of the ladder. Dig out a trench 9 feet in length by 2 feet wide.

3. A level will keep the bricks on an even keel. Use 31 bricks.

2. Begin to lay the bricks onto a dry mix base. Use a builder's line to insure a straight run.

4. Having completed the first "upright" of the ladder, the second can be laid parallel to the first and 4 bricks apart. Keep checking the distance between the "uprights" as the bricks are laid to make sure they are parallel.

5. Install the "rungs" of the ladder.

6. Lay the plants out for planting by following the Planting Plan.

1. Tease out the roots of each plant before you plant it.

In Section 1, plant the 6 chamomile plants (A). This variety of chamomile forms a low ground-hugging mat and is commonly used to create chamomile lawns. Here, it has been selected to offer a low contrast to the sage and rue in the second section, and to soften the brickwork at one end.

2. In Section 2, plant 1 golden sage (B). This sage has green and golden variegated leaves. It will grow out over the brickwork forming a low mound. The color and texture of the leaves will provide a good companion for the rue and the chives (in Section 3).

Next, plant the rue (C). This herb, used only for medicinal purposes, has great ornamental use. It combines well with roses and herbaceous plants. Here, its powder-blue, finely divided leaves provide a contrast in shape and texture to those of the accompanying sages. *Warning: handling this plant can cause an allergic reaction. Care should be taken not to touch the leaves when planting or collecting sage for the kitchen.*

In front of the rue, still in Section 2, plant 1 purple sage (D). This sage has purple leaves and the same form as the golden sage.

3. In Section 3, plant 1 chive (E). As well as being one of the best culinary herbs, the attractive chive flowers contribute much to any planting scheme. The grass-like leaves

Planting Plan

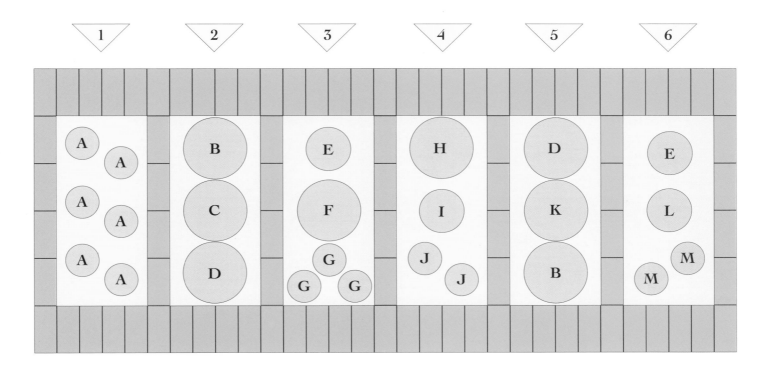

contrast well with the gray-leaved curry plant and the upright tarragon.

Next plant the tarragon (F). By planting it in the center, the surrounding plants will help to mask it later in the season when it can become very untidy. The plant produces invasive underground runners, and is, therefore, best planted in a large flowerpot or old bucket, with the bottom removed.

Plant the 3 golden feverfew (G) in a group. In the spring, nothing can compete with golden feverfew for its bright freshness. It loses some color as the season goes by, but trimming it over occasionally encourages fresh growth. Here it will contrast well with the purple sage in Section 2 and pick up the colors of the lemon thyme in Section 4.

4. In Section 4, plant the curry plant (H). Unlike many gray-leaved plants, the curry plant looks good all the year round. Here it will contrast with the feathery leaves of the bronze fennel and the textured leaves of the sage. Trimming the plant occasionally will encourage it to bush out.

Next, plant the bronze fennel (I). This perennial is commonly used in mixed flower borders where its tall feathery form offers a contrast to many border plants. Fennel attracts syrphid flies, a voracious predator of whitefly which has a taste for basil, and, thereby, makes a practical contribution to the garden, as well as a culinary and ornamental one.

Plant the 2 lemon thyme (J). This variety has a strong lemon scent and the bonus of pink flowers in midsummer. Here, the golden yellow leaves pick up the golden theme from the sage in Section 2 and Section 5, and the golden feverfew in Section 3.

There is a vast range of thymes, many of which are useful ornamentally, some in mixed borders and others in rockeries and paving.

5. In Section 5, plant the second purple sage (D). This helps provide balance throughout the scheme.

Plant the apple mint (K) next. This tall growing mint has large, oval, furry leaves, a contrast in texture to the sage and bronze

fennel. It produces underground spreading roots and is, therefore, best planted in a large bottomless flowerpot or old bucket, sunk into the ground.

Plant the second golden sage (B). The four sages in this scheme provide balance, structure, and winter color.

6. In Section 6, plant the remaining chives (E). Duplicating the grassy leaves of chives gives continuity throughout the scheme. Add 2 parsley (M), the feathery leaves of which are a good companion to other plants. Next, plant the basil (L). Basil comes in a range of varieties, some with purple leaves, and any of these would be suitable. In this case, the round, shiny leaves of the sweet basil contrast well with the apple mint and parsley. Basil is not a hardy plant, and should not be planted outside in colder areas until all risk of frost has passed.

7. The completed garden, if created in the spring, will take two or three months to mature.

ALTERNATIVE PLANTING SCHEME

This scheme includes a number of plants which are not reliably hardy. It will need a sheltered site in areas prone to winter frosts.

Section 1
A. 6 thyme (*Thymus serpyllum* "Annie Hall") 3½ inch pots

Section 2
B. 1 myrtle (*Myrtus communis* "Variegata"), 6½ inch or 7½ inch pot
C. 1 rosemary (*Rosmarinus officinalis*), 6½ inch or 7½ inch pot
D. 1 sage (*Salvia officinalis*), 6½ inch or 7½ inch pot

Section 3
E. 3 garlic (*Allium sativum*) 3½ inch pots
F. 1 lovage (*Levisticum officinale*), 3½ inch pot
G. 2 lady's mantle (*Alchemilla mollis*), 3½ inch pots

Section 4
H. 1 lavender (*Lavnandula angustifolia* "Munstead"), 6½ inch or 7½ inchpot
I. 1 apple mint (*Mentha suaveolens*), 6½ inch or 7½ inch pot
J. 1 lavender (*Lavandula angustifolia* "Munstead"), 6½ inch or 7½ inch pot

Section 5
D. 1 sage (*Salvia officinalis*) 6½ inch or 7½ inch pot

K. 1 variegated rue (*Ruta graveolens* "Variegata"), 5½ inch or 6½ inch pot
B. 1 sage (*Salvia officinalis*), 6½ inch or 7½ inch pot

Section 6
E. 3 garlic (*Allium sativum*), 3½ inch pots
L. 1 tricolored sage (*Salvia officinalis* "Tricolor"), 6½ inch or 7½ inch pot
M. 2 lady's mantle (*Alchemilla mollis*), 3½ inch pots

HERB POTS

Herbs are the perfect subjects for container gardening – their invasive tendency curtailed, and requiring little watering, they seem at home. It is easy to bring the herbs near the kitchen door or into the house at the end of the growing season for use in the winter months. Subjects like tarragon, which can look so untidy late in the season, can be hidden from view until the following year. Container groups are the ideal way of adding interest and maturity to a paved area. The common mistake is to dot them around a large area, where they make little impact and often cause an obstruction. Draw them together into groups, and place them strategically next to doorways or beside a sitting area.

The Plants

1 bay (Laurus nobilis), 6½ inch or 8½ inch

1 tarragon (Artemisia dracunculus), 5½ inch or 6½ inch pot

1 tricolored sage (Salvia officinalis "Tricolor"), 6½ inch pot

3 gold-splashed oregano (Origanum vulgare "Gold Tip"), 5½ inch pots

1 eau-de-Cologne mint (Mentha × piperita citrata), 5½ inch or 6½ inch pot

1 golden thyme (Thymus vulgaris aureus), 5½ inch pot

3 parsley (Petroselinum crispum), 5½ inch pots

1 chives (Allium schoenoprasum), 3½ inch or 5½ inch pot

Materials

Three terra-cotta flowerpots, one each of diameter 18 inches; 15½ inches; and 13 inches • 4 terra-cotta flowerpots, each 10½ inches in diameter • Crockery shards • Peat-based potting soil

115

Planting Plan

The parsley will need replacing annually, but the other plants will grow happily in their pots for up to three years with an annual top dressing of soil. Eventually, when a plant becomes too large, it could be planted into a larger container, or planted out into the garden.

During very hot weather, watering should be carried out at least twice a day, early in the morning and again in the evening. The pot should be watered until a puddle appears around the base of the pot. Feed with a liquid fertilizer every other week (each week for the parsley).

In colder climates, where prolonged frosts can be expected, the whole group should be moved to a sheltered part of the garden and given extra protection (the roots, being above ground, are more exposed to frost attack).

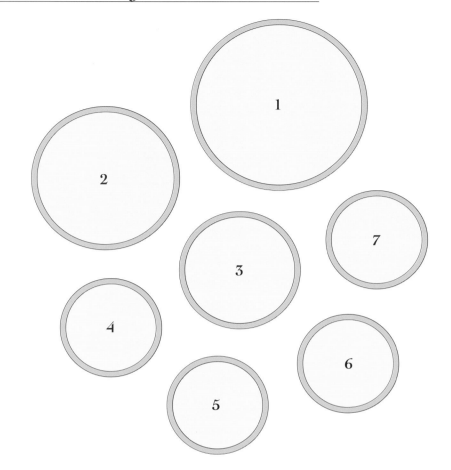

1. Start with the largest pot (Container 1). Cover the base of the container with a generous layer of crockery shards to aid drainage. Add the potting soil up to 1½ inches lower than the rim of the pot.

2. Remove the bay tree from its pot by inverting the plant and gently squeezing the rootball inside the plastic container. Tease the roots from the rootball to insure the plant grows away well. Make sure the plant is planted to the same level as in its original pot. Bay is not fully hardy, and should be protected during cold weather.

3. Plant 3 gold-splashed oregano plants, equally spaced around the edge of the container.

4. The oregano plants will quickly cover the bare soil in the pot, and even cascade down the sides.

5. The positioning of the group is critical to the overall effect. Here, the gravel sets the terra-cotta off nicely.

6. Plant Container 2 with the tarragon and place alongside the first. Plant eau de cologne mint in Container 3 to make a striking contrast. This group is attractive on its own, and you may wish not to add further containers.

7. Plant 3 parsley plants in Container 4; a tricolored sage in Container 5; golden thyme in Container 6; and chives in Container 7. Place these carefully around the outside of the group. The plants will need about two weeks in which to mature enough to harvest, and two months to reach full maturity.

ALTERNATIVE PLANTING SCHEME

Container 1
1 rosemary (*Rosmarinus officinalis* "Miss Jessop's Upright"), 6½ inch pot
3 prostrate thyme (*Thymus serpyllum* "Pink Chintz"), 3½ inch pots

Container 2
1 apple mint (*Mentha suaveolens*), 5½ inch or 6½ inch pot

Container 3
1 rue (*Ruta graveolens* "Jackman's Blue"), 6½ inch pot

Container 4
1 basil (*Ocimum basilicum* "Green Ruffles"), 3½ inch or 5½ inch pot

Container 5
1 lady's mantle (*Alchemilla mollis*), 3½ inch or 5½ inch pot

Container 6
1 purple sage (*Salvia officinalis* "Purpurascens"), 6½ inch or 7½ inch pot

Container 7
2 flat-leaf parsley (*Petroselinum crispum hortense*), 3½ inch pots

MINT DIAMONDS

*T*here are very many different varieties of mint now available, but nearly all are aggressive colonizers and require some method to segregate them. The diamond pattern of bricks not only looks good, but also helps to constrain the plants. The bold pattern of this feature may dominate the design of the garden in the near vicinity, so care must be taken in placing it. It would fit well into a patio, where the bricks could be used to pick up the color of the bricks in the house, and as a dominant feature, it is particularly appropriate in a large paved area. It could also look good in a scree bed or gravel garden, with stepping stones through the gravel for access.

Materials

144 bricks • Lean mix (6 parts builder's sand to 1 part cement) • Builder's line • Level • Brick hammer • Spade • Bricklayer's trowel • Garden trowel

CARE

An occasional trim when the herbs are in flower will help to keep the plants' shapes and stop any seed being set.

The Plants

2 spearmint (Mentha spicata), 5½ ich or 6½ inch pots

2 eau-de-cologne mint (Mentha x piperita citrata), 5½ inch or 6½ inch pots

2 pineapple mint (Mentha suaveolens "Variegata"), 5½ inch or 6½ inch pots

1 apple mint (Mentha suaveolens), 5½ inch or 6½ inch pot

1. Dig out a trench 2 feet wide and 1 foot deep.

2. Lay the first layer of bricks on a generous layer of lean mix, in the pattern shown. Use a builder's line to insure a straight line.

3. Lay three layers of brick. The roots of mints are very invasive, and the deeper you can go, the better. Three layers should be enough, but to make sure, go one or two layers deeper. It is essential that all the bricks are carefully pointed up, or an escape route will be provided for the plants.

4. When the bricks have been laid, lay out the plants ready to be planted.

Planting Plan

ALTERNATIVE PLANTING SCHEME

This planting uses popular culinary herbs.

Diamond 1.
1 eau-de-cologne mint (*Mentha × piperita citrata*), 5½ inch or 6½ inch pot

Diamond 2.
5 parsley (*Petroselinum crispum*), 3½ inch pots

Diamond 3.
5 lemon thyme (*Thymus × citriodorus* "Silver Posie"), 3½ inch pots

Diamond 4.
1 rosemary (*Rosmarinus officinalis*), 5½ inch or 6½ inch pot

Diamond 5.
4 basil (*Ocimum basilicum*), 3½ inch pots

Diamond 6.
5 chives (*Allium schoenoprasum*), 3½ inch pots

Diamond 7
1 purple sage (*Salvia officinalis* "Purpurascens"), 5½ inch or 6½ inch pot

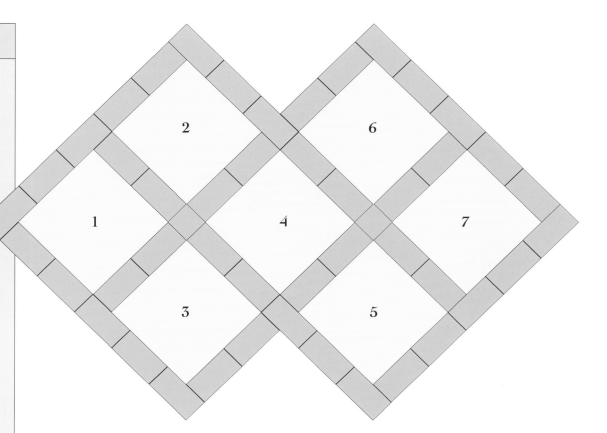

1. Break each plant out of its pot by inverting it and squeezing the plastic pot. Before planting, tease the roots out from the rootball to make sure the plant grows away well. In Diamond 1, plant one spearmint.

2. Plant one of the variegated pineapple mints in Diamond 2; and one of the fragrant eau-de-cologne mints in Diamond 3.

3. In Diamond 4, plant the apple mint, and in Diamond 5, the second pineapple mint.

4. In Diamond 6, plant the second eau-de-cologne mint. Finally, plant the other spearmint plant in Diamond 7.

5. After planting, it will take two or three months for the scheme to take shape.

ALTERNATIVE PLANTING SCHEME

Diamond 1.
1 basil mint
(*Mentha × piperita citrata* "Basil"),
5½ inch or 6½ inch pot

Diamond 2.
1 Moroccan mint
(*Mentha spicata* "Moroccan"),
5½ inch or 6½ inch pot

Diamond 3.
1 European pennyroyal (*Mentha pulegium*), 5½ inch pot

Diamond 4.
1 ginger mint
(*Mentha × gentilis*),
5½ inch or 6½ inch pot

Diamond 5.
1 curly mint
(*Mentha spicata crispa*), 5½ inch pot

Diamond 6.
1 European pennyroyal (*Mentha pulegium*), 5½ inch pot

Diamond 7
1 black peppermint
(*Mentha × piperita*),
5½ inch or 6½ inch pot

HERB WHEEL

◦

*T*his traditional design is a simple, but very effective, way of growing herbs, and is often used as the central feature

in an ornamental vegetable or kitchen garden. An attractive idea is to place a small sundial, birdbath, or small statue in the center.

The Plants

A. *3 golden oregano (Origanum vulgare "Aureum"), 3½ inch pots*

B. *2 lemon thyme (Thymus × citriodorus "Silver Posie"), 3½ inch pots*

C. *2 chives (Allium schoenoprasum), 3½ inch pots*

D. *4 parsley (Petroselinum crispum), 3½ inch pots*

E. *1 basil (Ocimum basilicum), 3½ inch or 5½ inch pot*

F. *1 pineapple mint (Mentha suaveolens "Variegata"), 5½ inch or 6½ inch pot*

Materials

71 bricks • Lean mix (6 parts builder's sand to 1 part cement) • Builder's line • Level • Brick hammer • Spade • Bricklayer's trowel • Garden trowel • Stake

G. *3 golden thyme (Thymus vulgaris aureus), 3½ inch pots*

H. *1 Corsican rosemary (Rosmarinus officinalis "Corsican Blue"), 6½ inch or 7½ inch pot*

I. *1 coriander (Coriandum sativum), 3½ inch or 5½ inch cm pot*

J. *1 black peppermint (Mentha × piperita), 6½ inch or 8½ inch pot*

1. Drive a stake into the ground and loosely attach a 30 inch length of builder's line. Using the metal marker at the other end of the line, carefully mark out the inner circle of the wheel "rim."

2. Dig out a shallow trench, and line with a lean cement mix.

4. Once the "rim" has been laid, mark out the "spokes" and line these with the lean cement mix. Lay the bricks as shown.

3. Lay bricks, using the builder's line to make sure the circle is followed. Check that each brick is even using a level.

5. Lay the plants out on the completed wheel in their positions, ready for planting, by following the Planting Plan.

Start to plant • HERB GARDENS

Planting Plan

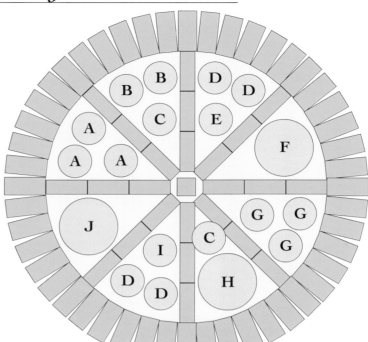

ALTERNATIVE PLANTING SCHEME

1st Section
A. 3 wild strawberry (*Fragaria vesca*),
3½ inch pots

2nd Section
B. 2 prostrate thyme (*Thymus
serpyllum* "Annie Hall"),
3½ inch pots
C. 1 garlic chives (*Allium tuberosum*),
3½ inch pot

3rd Section
D. 2 parsley (*Petroselinum crispum*),
3½ inch pots
E. 1 cinnamon basil (*Ocimum basilicum*
"Cinnamon"), 3½ inch or 5½ inch pot

4th Section
F. 1 prostrate rosemary (*Rosmarinus
lavandulaceus*), 6½ inch or 7½ inch pot

5th Section
G. 3 alpine strawberry (*Fragaria vesca*
"Semperflorens"), 3½ inch pots

6th Section
C. 1 tree onion (*Allium cepa proliferum*),
3½ inch pot
H. 1 lavender (*Lavandula angustifolia*
"Hidcote"), 5½ inch or 6½ inch pot

7th Section
I. 1 chervil (*Anthriscus cerefolium*),
3½ inch pot
D. 2 parsley (*Petroselinum crispum*),
3½ inch pots

8th Section
J. 1 purple sage (*Salvia officinalis*
"Purpurascens"), 6½ inch or 7½ inch
pot

1. To remove each plant from its pot, invert it gently and squeeze the pot. Tease out the roots before planting because this encourages the plant to grow away quickly.

Start by planting the 3 golden oregano (A) in one of the "wedges." The golden leaves will contrast well with the black peppermint, which will be planted in the neighboring section.

2. In the next section, plant 2 thymes (B) and 1 chive (C). The small variegated leaves of the thymes add freshness to the scheme. The grass-like leaves of the chives are essential in any scheme, adding contrasting shape. The flowers, which bloom all summer if deadheaded regularly, associate well with many color schemes.

3. Plant 2 parsley (D) and 1 basil (E) in the next section. The parsley associates well with the neighboring plants, and the basil adds freshness to the scheme – its round leaves contrasting well with the grass-like leaves of the chives.

4. The pineapple mint (F) is planted in the next section. This variegated plant adds texture and shape, and complements the variegation in the thyme.

5. Next plant the 3 golden thymes (G) in the neighboring sections. These are chosen to balance the golden oregano in the opposite section of the wheel.

6. In the section next to the golden thymes, plant the other chive plant (C), to add continuity through the plan, and the Corsican rosemary (H). This low-growing rosemary will grow out over the "rim" of the wheel, as well as offer a contrast to the golden thyme and chives.

7. The 2 remaining parsley (D) and the coriander (I) are planted in the next "wedge." The deeply divided coriander leaves will balance the parsley growing in the opposite section and complement the parsley growing beside it.

8. Plant the black peppermint (J), or the similar eau-de-cologne mint, to add a welcome color contrast. Like all mints, this plant is invasive, so plant it inside a bottomless flowerpot or bucket with a depth of not less than 12 inches.

9. The final scheme will take two to three months to develop, if planted in the spring.

CARE

Parsley, basil, and coriander are all annuals, and will need replacing each year. The basil and coriander are both tender, and should not be planted in cold areas until after the danger of frost has passed. The parsley and basil will benefit from the occasional liquid feed.

HERBS IN PAVING

Paving offers ideal conditions for growing the many herbs that prefer hot, dry conditions, and leaves brushed against or crushed by passing feet release their heady aromas into the air. The checkerboard pattern, used in this project, could be replicated throughout a patio by using light and darker colored slabs. The stepping stone route through this herb bed could be reorganized into a more straightforward route through the herbs, or other interesting designs for a path could be developed.

Materials

Six 18 inch, square paving slabs

• Hardcore rubble • Concrete cement mix • Level • Bricklayer's trowel • Garden trowel • Brick hammer

CARE

Trimming over the thyme in the spring is all that should be required, unless the sage becomes leggy, then this should be cut back hard.

The Plants

A. *1 Moroccan mint (Mentha spicata "Moroccan"), 5½ inch or 6½ inch pot*

B. *3 oregano (Origanum vulgare), 5½ inch pots*

C. *1 tricolored sage (Salvia officinalis "Tricolor"), 6½ inch or 8½ inch pot*

D. *2 thyme (Thymus "Doone Valley"), 5½ inch pots*

E. *4 chamomile (Chamaemelum nobile "Treneague"), 3½ inch pots*

F. *4 Corsican mint (Mentha requienii), 3½ inch pots*

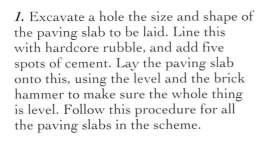

1. Excavate a hole the size and shape of the paving slab to be laid. Line this with hardcore rubble, and add five spots of cement. Lay the paving slab onto this, using the level and the brick hammer to make sure the whole thing is level. Follow this procedure for all the paving slabs in the scheme.

2. Lay the plants in position, ready for planting, following the Planting Plan.

Planting Plan

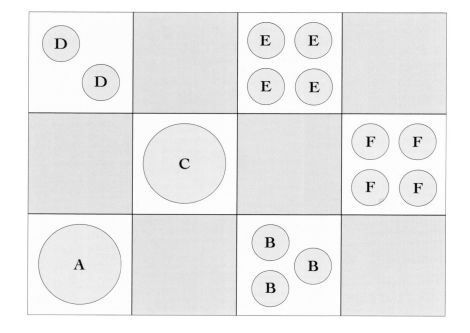

1. Remove each plant from its pot by first inverting the plant, and then carefully squeezing the outside. Tease the roots out to make sure the plant grows away well, before planting.

Plant the Moroccan mint (A) in the bottom left-hand square, and the 3 oregano (B) in the square next to it. Plant the tricolored sage (C) in the center square.

2. Plant the 2 thymes (D) in the top left-hand square, the 4 chamomile (E) in the square next to the thymes, and the 4 Corsican mints (F) in the remaining square.

3. The finished project will take 2 or 3 months
to develop, if planted in the spring.

HANGING BASKET

Hanging baskets full of lobelia, ivy-leaved geraniums, impatiens, and trailing fuchsias have become a popular summer feature. A hanging basket of herbs is not only attractive, but very *useful, and can be brought into the kitchen and hung from a hook whenever culinary herbs are needed. Many of the herbs are evergreen, so this basket can be used all year round.*

Materials

A hanging basket, 23½ inches in diameter • Moss • A square of plastic sheet, perforated for drainage • Peat-based potting soil

CARE

Hanging baskets dry out very quickly, so they cannot be overwatered. In warm weather, they will require watering at least three times a day. A good method of watering is to use a large, plastic soft-drink bottle and a chair to stand on (and then to sit on when the job is done!). Wind can have a severe desiccating effect, and in severe conditions, the hanging basket should be removed to a sheltered spot.

The plants used here can only stay in the hanging basket for a season (one year, if planted in the spring and brought in the house for winter). Some of the plants can be planted out into the garden after the basket is finished.

The Plants

A. *2 purple sage (Salvia officinalis "Purpurascens"), 3½ inch pots*

B. *2 parsley (Petroselinum crispum), 3½ inch pots*

C. *2 oregano (Origanum vulgare "Gold Tip"), 3½ inch pots*

D. *1 rosemary (Rosmarinus officinalis), 5½ inch pot*

E. *1 chives (Allium schoenoprasum), 3½ inch or 5½ inch pot*

F. *2 lemon thyme (Thymus × citriodorus "Silver Posie"), 3½ inch pots*

GARDEN MATTERS

G. *1 basil (Ocimum basilicum), 3½ inch pot*

1. Stand the hanging basket in a medium-size flowerpot to hold it steady and upright.

2. Line the base with moss, bringing it about a third of the way up the basket side. Make sure the moss is well consolidated.

3. Cut a plastic sheet from the soil bag. Place the plastic sheeting in the base of the basket. This will help to keep moisture in and prevent the basket from drying out too quickly.

Planting Plan

1. Position the first layer of plants in their growing position. Tease the roots out to encourage good root development. Plant 2 purple sage (A), 2 parsley (B), and 2 oregano (C) in positions shown in the Planting Plan.

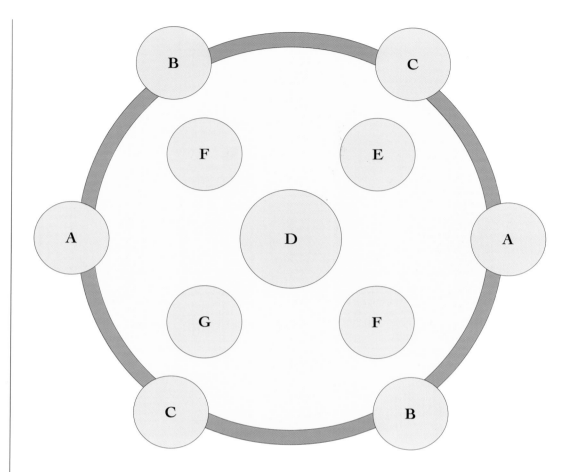

2. Build the moss up around the sides to the top of the basket.

3. Add potting soil into the center of the "nest" created by the moss.

4. Plant 1 rosemary (D), 1 chive (E), 2 thymes (F), and 1 basil (G) in the positions shown in the Planting Plan.

ALTERNATIVE PLANTING SCHEME

This unusual planting scheme requires longer wires to support the basket, in order to allow room for the fennel to grow. It can be controlled by simply cutting the top off periodically.

A. 2 golden feverfew (*Chrysanthemum parthenium* "Aureum"), 3½ inch pots

B. 2 coriander (*Coriandrum sativum*), 3½ inch pots

C. 2 wild strawberry (*Fragaria vesca*), 3½ inch pots

D. 1 tarragon (*Artemisia dracunculus*), 3½ inch pot

E. 1 chives (*Allium schoenoprasum*), 3½ inch or 5½ inch pot

F. 2 bronze fennel (*Foeniculum vulgare* "Purpureum"), 3½ inch or 5½ inch pots

G. 1 curry plant (*Helichrysum italicum*), 3½ inch or 5½ inch pot

5. The finished basket will take a few weeks to mature to the point where the herbs can be harvested for the kitchen.

HERB BORDER

◦○◦

*T*his herb border should be south- or south-west facing, and backed by a fence or wall. If the herbs are to be fully utilized, they should be grown within easy reach of where they will be needed, usually the kitchen.

The herb garden's inherent untidiness could spoil the view of the garden, but by carefully selecting the plants, and positioning them with care in the border, the herbs will blend together, or with other garden plants, to create an attractive planted border.

The Plants

A. *3 variegated wild strawberry (Fragaria vesca "Variegata"), 3½ inch pots*

B. *1 chives (Allium schoenoprasum), 3½ inch or 5½ inch pot*

C. *5 sweet cicely (Myrrhis odorata), 3½ inch pots*

D. *7 catnip (Nepeta racemosa, syn. Nepeta mussinii), 3½ inch pots*

E. *1 angelica (Angelica archangelica), 3½ inch or 5½ inch pot*

CARE

This scheme will need little maintenance and should give pleasure for a number of years before any changes are needed.

If the sage looks a little "leggy" in the spring, cut it back hard. The artemisia must be cut to within 2 inches of the ground every spring as soon as growth appears and close to the base. If not, then it will grow "birds nests" on the end of each branch, and become large and untidy. Trim the catnip with a pair of shears when the flowers have finished, and it will flower again (the plant can be encouraged to flower all summer).

F. *2 bee balms (Monarda didyma "Cambridge* Scarlet"), 3½ inch pots*

G. *1 iris (Iris foetidissima "Variegata"), 5½ inch or 6½ inch pot*

H. *1 pineapple mint (Mentha suaveolens "Variegata"), 5½ inch or 6½ inch pot*

S1. *2 rosemary (Rosmarinus officinalis), 6½ inch or 7½ inch pots*

Materials

Garden spade • Rake • Garden trowel
• Wheelbarrow • Vine eyes
• Galvanized wire

S2. *2 purple sage (Salvia officinalis "Purpurascens"), 6½ inch or 8½ inch pots*

GRAHAM A. PAVEY

S3. *2 rue (Ruta graveolens "Jackman's Blue"), 5½ inch or 6½ inch pots*

S4. *1 golden sage (Salvia officinalis "Icterina") 6½ inch or 8½ inch pot*

S5. *1 artemisia (Artemisia "Powis Castle"), 5½ inch or 6½ inch pot*

1. Dig over the area to be planted (about 16 feet x 8 feet), to one spade's depth, incorporating sharp sand (¼ inch spread across the surface before digging in). Rake over the surface to form a fine tilth.

Planting Plan

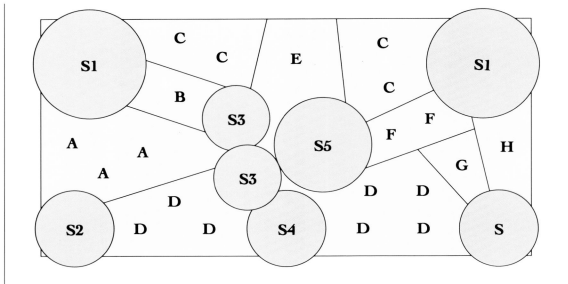

1. First, plant the structural plants. Some are evergreen and provide all-year-round color to the scheme. Pick out the key points first, in this case the corners, with the structural plants. Plant the 2 rosemary (S1) and the 2 purple sage (S2) in the corners, as shown on the Planting Plan. Then fill out the central area with the 2 rue (S3), a golden sage (S4), and the artemisia (S5).

2. When planting, make sure the roots are teased out so the plants grow away well.

3. Plant up the first layer of infill plants. The 7 catnip (D) will flower for most of the summer, if trimmed over occasionally with a pair of shears. It compliments the sage at each corner, and contrasts well with the golden sage planted in the center. The rue has a fine blue finish to its leaves, which picks up the blue of the catnip and carries it through the scheme. The variegation in the pineapple mint (H) adds a bright contrast. Plant it in a bottomless flowerpot or bucket.

4. The second layer of infill planting completes the plan, and includes some of the larger plants. Angelica (E) will grow to 5 feet or more, and has been given plenty of room at the back of the border. The feathery leaves of the 5 sweet cicely (C) infill nicely between the tall angelica and the medium level. The 3 variegated wild strawberry (A) balance the variegated apple mint on the opposite side of the border. The sword leaves of the iris (G) add impact on the right, and are picked up by the grass-like leaves of the chives (B) on the left. The plan is finished with a bold splash of red provided by the flowers of the 2 wild bergamot (F).

5. When the border has been planted up, mulching between plants will keep weeds down, maintain moisture, and provide a background for the plants. In this instance, forest bark has been used, but peasize shingle would work equally well and may be more appropriate, depending on the overall design. The ground must be thoroughly wetted before mulch is applied. Because it acts as insulation, it can just as easily keep the ground bone-dry as it can keep it moist. Also, it must be a fair depth (2 inches, ideally) to insure any weed seeds are kept in the dark and, therefore, do not germinate.

6. The final scheme will mature quite quickly if planted in the spring or early summer.

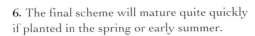

HERBS IN A MIXED BORDER

Herbs are fine plants for a mixed border, so why allocate them a separate garden? This project explores how herbs can be used in a border with other flowering plants. It is an excellent way of growing herbs within an overall garden scene. Any herbs not grown in the border can be

grown in pots on the patio. The border is 25 feet long by about 9 feet deep and should ideally be south- or west-facing. If your border is east-facing, then it could also be used, as long as it is backed by a 6 foot high fence and not a tall house wall or high hedge.

The Plants

S1. *2 santolina (Santolina chamaecyparissus), 6½ inch pots*

S2. *2 Mexican orange blossom (Choisya ternata), 7½ inch pots or bigger*

S3. *2 sage (Salvia officinalis), 6½ inch or 7½ inch pots*

S4. *1 California lilac (Ceanothus thyrsiflorus), 7½ inch pot or bigger*

S5. *6 lavender (Lavandula angustifolia), 5½ inch or 6½ inch pots*

S6. *1 rosemary (Rosmarinus officinalis), 6½ inch or 7½ inch pot*

A. *3 bee balms (Monarda didyma), 3½ inch pots*

B. *3 chives (Allium schoenoprasum), 3½ inch or 5½ inch pots*

C. *2 cranesbill (Geranium × riversleaianum "Russell Prichard"), 5½ inch or 6½ inch pots*

D. *2 fennel (Foeniculum vulgare), 3½ inch or 5½ inch pots*

E. *1 spearmint (Mentha spicata), 5½ inch or 6½ inch pot*

Materials

Garden spade • Rake • Garden trowel
• Galvanized wire • Vine screw eyes

F. *2 heuchera (Heuchera "Palace Purple"), 3½ inch or 5½ inch pots*

G. *2 parsley (Petroselinum crispum), 3½ inch pots*

H. *2 iris (Iris pallida "Variegata"), 3½ inch or 5½ inch pots*

I. *2 euphorbia (Euphorbia characias wulfenii), 3½ inch or 5½ inch pots*

J. *3 lady's mantle (Alchemilla mollis), 3½ inch pots*

K. *1 pineapple mint (Mentha suaveolens "Variegata"), 5½ inch or 6½ inch pot*

L. *1 tarragon (Artemisia dracunculus), 3½ inch or 5½ inch pot*

K1. *1 juniper (Juniperus communis "Hibernica"), 7½ inch pot or bigger*

C1. *2 grapevines (Vitis vinifera "Black Hamburg"), 6½ inch or 7½ inch pots*

1. Dig over the area to be planted to one spade's depth.

2. Incorporate a mixture of peat, well-rotted farmyard manure (or compost), and sharp sand in equal parts (put a layer ¼ inch deep, spread across the surface, before digging in). Rake over the surface of the soil to form a fine tilth.

3. Vines always require support, and this can best be achieved by using vine screw eyes and galvanized wire. Either screw the vine eyes into the fence posts, or attach to a wall by drilling holes and inserting masonry plugs. Galvanized wire should then be stretched horizontally between the eyes. The wire should be 18 inches apart vertically. This is the best form of support because it blends with the vine, allowing you to enjoy the plant and what is keeping it in place.

1. Plant the main structural plants – the "bones" of the scheme. These are the evergreens, which will provide all-year-round interest, and include 2 Mexican orange blossom (S2), a California lilac (S4), 2 sage (S3), and 2 santolinas (S1).

2. Plant the infill structural plants. When the key structural plants have been planted, the smaller evergreens are used to insure a good spread throughout the scheme. The 2 grapevines (C1) on the back fence or wall, although not evergreen, will grow thick, wooly stems in time, and these will add winter interest, along with the juniper (K1), the rosemary (S6), and 6 lavenders (S5). The upright shape of the juniper is an important contrast for the round shape of the California lilac, and adds height to the overall scheme.

Planting Plan

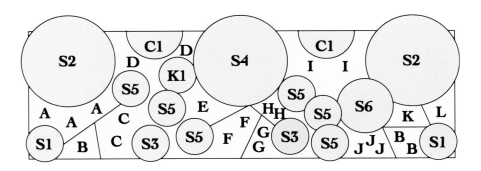

4. The final group of infill plants includes 3 chives (B), whose flowers can be used to brighten up a salad, and the feathery foliage of the 2 parsley (G) which, as an annual, will need replacing each year. The spearmint (E) and the pineapple mint (K) should be planted in a large bottomless flowerpot or bucket to contain their invasive roots. Plant the variegated iris (H) and the cranesbills (C) in the border. The cranesbills will flower their heart out all summer long, and they combine well with the form and flower color of chives, an excellent front-of-the-border perennial.

3. Smaller herbaceous perennials and shrubs, grown for their flowers and color, are planted around the structural plants to add flair. This first group will bring in rich reds with the bee balm (A) and deep purple with the heucheras (F).

The tarragon (L) should be planted in a large bottomless flowerpot or bucket to prevent its invasive runners spreading too far. Plant the 2 fennel (D), the 2 euphorbia (I), and the 2 lady's mantle (J).

5. After planting, the scheme will take three or four months to establish itself (if planted in the spring) and about four years to mature.

CARE

Trim the santolina and lavender, after flowering, with large pruning shears to maintain shape. Tie new growth from the grapevines into wires in late summer or fall. Remove dead foliage each spring. Replace the parsley annually.

WINDOW BOX

*H*erbs need to be close at hand for the creative cook, and having them just outside the kitchen window is the perfect solution. They can easily be looked after in this situation and, as long as they are well watered and replaced when too big, a large number can be grown in a small space. Try a window box at each window, perhaps adding a similar geranium into each window box to provide continuity.

The Plants

1 pineapple mint (Mentha suaveolens "Variegata"), 5½ inch or 6½ inch pot

1 rosemary (Rosmarinus officinalis), 6½ inch pot

1 lemon thyme (Thymus × citriodorus "Silver Posie"), 3½ inch pot

1 purple sage (Salvia officinalis "Purpurascens"), 6½ inch pot

1 oregano (Origanum vulgare "Gold Tip"), 3½ inch pot

2 parsley (Petroselinum crispum), 3½ inch pots

1 chives (Allium schoenoprasum), 3½ inch pot

Materials

A window box, 30 inches × 7 inches high × 8 inches • Crockery shards • Peat-based potting soil • Garden trowel

CARE

Because the plants are crammed in for effect, they can remain in the container for one year (if planted in spring and brought indoors in winter). The perennials and shrubs could be planted out into the garden.

1. Put a layer of shards to cover the bottom of the container.

2. Add the potting soil to about 1½ inches lower than the top of the container.

3. Lay the plants out roughly in the position they are to grow.

Planting Plan

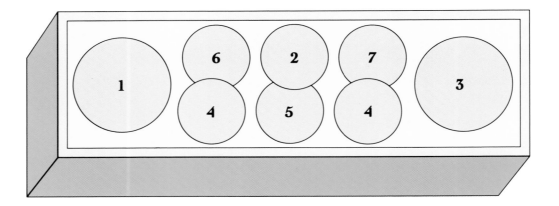

1. Plant the main plants first. In this case, the mint, sage, and rosemary. Remove each plant from its plastic pot by gently squeezing the pot. Tease out the roots of each before planting. Plant the pineapple mint in Area 1; the rosemary in Area 2; and the purple sage in Area 3.

2. Plant the "infill" plants to complete the arrangement: a parsley plant in each Area 4; the thyme in Area 5; the oregano in Area 6; and finally the chives in Area 7.

ROCK & ALPINE GARDENS

Create natural settings for unusual
alpine plants, using a variety of
rocks, pebbles, and stone sinks

INTRODUCTION

G rowing wild in the mountain ranges of the world are some of our loveliest garden plants – alpines. These rock and scree plants grow at high altitudes above the timberline, but the term "alpine" is loosely used to include a vast range of low-growing rock-garden plants, including many bulbs, that may be grown successfully at relatively low altitudes.

The term "alpine" also gives an indication of how we should grow these plants, but how we display them, like many other forms of gardening, changes as time passes. With today's more integrated approach to gardening, with more emphasis on the natural overall look of the whole garden, alpines and rock garden plants can be introduced into any size of garden to provide a wealth of beautiful species.

BILL SHAW

GRAHAM A PAVEY

Most are amenable and undemanding plants that will grow readily in a suitably prepared site in the garden. Not only rockeries, but areas of pebbles, stones, or cobblestones are attractive ways of growing alpines. Like cracks in paving and walls, they simulate wild conditions and allow the alpine or rock garden to become integrated into the overall design of the garden.

Rockeries are an excellent way of exploring the fascinating world of alpines. Even a tiny rock garden can accommodate many of these delightful plants, and different environments can be constructed to grow a range of species. Alpine plants are perfect for container gardening, and a miniature rock garden in a raised bed is an ideal option where space is limited. From sink gardens to hanging baskets, alpines can be used to create an all-year-round interest that is easy to maintain and requires minimum attention.

MATERIALS AND TECHNIQUES

Pea-size pebbles

Materials for Projects

Bricks come in a range of hardness, from very soft molded bricks to very hard engineering bricks. The softer the brick, the more prone it is to attack by frost, but it may have a more attractive texture than a harder one. Frost-damaged bricks can be a feature in themselves.

Cement is used for making hyper-tufa and for construction work.

Horticultural gravel is used as a mulch around plants in a finished rock garden. It keeps plants clean, and the soil cool and moist around plant roots.

Lean mix is a mix of 6 parts sand to 1 part of cement with the addition of a little water to damp it down slightly, making it easier to use. When laid, it will dry to make a solid base.

Pea-size pebbles are used for the surface of scree beds, as a mulch, and for lining the base of stone troughs. The grade should be no more than ½ inch in size.

Stone chips are small pieces of natural stone, used as an alternative to sandstone pebbles, river pebbles, or gravel where it might fit better with the local stone.

Crockery shards

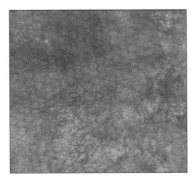

Mulching mat

Tufa

Crockery shards provide drainage in the base of containers. They are usually broken flowerpots or tiles, but large stones or pebbles could be used.

A **mulching mat**, usually made from an openweave, man-made material, is useful for maintaining moisture in the ground and keeping weeds under control.

Tufa is a very light, unusual material. Despite its appearance, it is not a rock, but a limestone deposit laid down by water which has passed through limestone rock.

145

Types of Rock

When deciding what type of rock to use for a rock garden, the first choice should be indigenous stone, which will look more natural than anything else.

A visit to your local garden center will indicate which rocks are available.

Granite *is a very hard stone in a range of colors, depending on its original location. This shiny material looks out of place if used in a limestone or sandstone region.*

Sandstone *is a very soft material, not ideal for use in a rock garden because it tends to quickly disintegrate. However, if it is your local stone, then consider using it and replacing it when necessary.*

Limestone *is available in a wide range. Much of it is very soft and has a tendency to suffer frost damage, but there are a number of very hard limestones, for example "Purbeck," which are hard enough to use as paving stones.*

Soil

Sharp sand

An **alpine planting mix** can be made by mixing two parts potting soil with one part sharp sand and a generous sprinkling of bonemeal.

Bonemeal

Sphagnum peatmoss is the best choice for creating hypertufa. Because the extraction of this material has an impact on the environment, use only a type from a managed source.

Yorkstone is a form of sandstone that makes a perfect paving material. It is also a good choice for rock outcrops and stone walls.

*Unusual **granite** egg-shaped and spherical stones are frequently dug out of gravel pits and tossed to one side. They are useful for creating attractive effects in a scree bed and flower border.*

Flint stones are useful, loosely laid, to create texture in a scree bed, or as an alternative to gravel around plants in a paved area.

Garden Equipment

A **garden broom** should be used for cleaning soil from paving stones and brickwork.

A **garden fork** is used for preparing the ground for planting. It is useful for breaking up any large clods of earth.

Garden gloves are useful when handling rocks, or even soil, when it is essential to protect the hands. Tough gardening gloves are ideal.

A **garden trowel** is needed for making small holes for planting.

Use a **garden hose** for filling the water tank in the bubble fountain project and for watering larger areas with a sprinkler attachment.

A **rake** is used to prepare the ground for planting. Draw it backward and forward across the soil until a fine tilth and level ground is achieved.

Use a **spade** for mixing soil and cement, and for digging holes.

Use a **watering can** for watering plants after planting when they require a good drenching to remove any air pockets from around the roots, and to give them a good start. This is best done with a watering can or hose, with a fine spray attachment. Continue to water daily for two or three weeks after planting. The evening or early in the morning are the best times to water.

A **wheelbarrow** is essential for transporting soil and rockery material with the least effort.

Project Equipment and Tools

A **bricklayer's line** consists of two metal stakes and strong cord, and is used for insuring a straight line when laying bricks.

A **bricklayer's trowel** is essential for laying and pointing between bricks.

A **masonry chisel** is used for breaking corners off paving slabs.

An **electric drill** is used for making holes in the tufa in which to plant. An ordinary household drill is ideal.

Galvanized wire frames, used for reinforcing concrete and other building and construction tasks, are ideal for supporting cobblestones in bubble fountains.

The handle of a **brick hammer** is used to tap paving slabs level when laying them in place.

An **old paintbrush** is needed to paint PVA adhesive onto the side of an old-fashioned sink in the stone-sink project.

Use a **level** to make sure paving or brickwork is laid straight.

A **submersible water pump**, which is larger than your requirements, is best because the flow of water can then be adjusted accordingly.

A **water tank**, 20 inches deep by 26 inches diameter, made of plastic or fiberglass, such as those usually used in lofts or attics, is needed for the bubble fountain project.

ROCK OUTCROP

This rock garden is designed to simulate an outcrop of rock, and will look most natural in an area where this phenomenon occurs naturally. It is part of an overall scheme, but a simple design of this size would make a fine feature on its own, perhaps with a wall or fence as a backdrop. The front of the rock garden could be combined with a scree bed or rock pavement.

The Plants

Here green-, yellow-, and variegated-leaf sedums and saxifrages form neat mounds with pink, red, white, and yellow flowers in spring and summer, while a juniper, a pale blue-flowered rosemary, and the rosettes of a house-leek provide low-growing, evergreen foliage. The delightful flowers of dianthus, lewisia, oxalis, and primroses in white, pink, and red shades contrast with the dark blue flowers of the veronica.

1

Saxifraga "White Pixie"

3

2 Sedum acre var. *aureum*

4

Saxifraga "Hi-Ace"

5

2 Saxifraga "Peter Pan"

6

Lewisia cotyledon hybrids

7

Rosmarinus officinalis "Severn Sea"

9

Saxifraga "Cloth of Gold"

10

Juniperus communis "Barton"

2 *Sedum album* "Coral Carpet"

8 *Dianthus* "La Bourboule Albus"

12 *Sempervivum tectorum* (Houseleek)

Materials

Alpine planting mix (see page 147) • Selected rockery stone in a variety of sizes • Garden trowel • Bricklayer's trowel • Heavy-duty gloves

Flowering Season

April to May.

2 Veronica peduncularis "Georgia Blue"

2 Primula denticulata alba

Oxalis adenophylla

2 Primula rosea grandiflora

Planting Plan

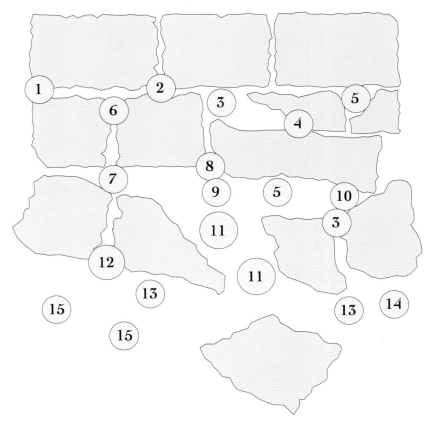

1. In certain areas, rock strata come to the surface, and it is this naturally occurring outcrop that is the origin of the garden rockery. When creating a rock garden of this nature, try to create something which simulates this and looks as natural as possible. This style of rock garden should be considered in an area where outcrops occur naturally, so it will appear truly natural, but careful positioning of stones will also create a suitably natural effect.

2. The stones used for this project may be too large to move comfortably. Use rounded fence stakes or wooden boards as runners to move them around.

3. Install the larger stones at the back, always trying to create an effect which simulates rock on the side of a mountain or outcrop. For strata appearing at the surface, like that shown in step 1, angle the stone at 45

degrees. It is important that the same angle is used throughout. Before placing a stone, look at the strata lines in the stone, and try to make these parallel throughout the arrangement.

4. When placing the stones, make sure that enough space is created between and around them for planting the alpines and rock plants.

5. Generally, alpines grow in well-drained, loose, stony areas on the side of mountains. It is essential, where possible, to simulate this, so backfill each planting space with drainage material, such as broken bricks, stones, and gravel.

CARE
Very little care is needed. Remove any flower heads after flowering.

6. Carefully fill each pocket with alpine planting mixture, slowly consolidating the mixture into any nooks or crannies by stopping periodically and firming well.

7. Following the Planting Plan, lay the plants out in their final position before planting. Remove each plant from its plastic pot by inverting it and gently squeezing the outside of the container. When removed from the pot, gently tease out the roots for planting. Dig a hole large enough for each plant, using your hand or a garden trowel.

8. Lewisias are perfectly frost-hardy, but detest winter moisture sitting in the crown of their leaves. To overcome this, they are best planted at an angle in the rock to allow rainwater to drain away.

9. After planting, spread pea-size pebbles, gravel or stone chips around the plants. This not only looks good, but also improves the drainage and reduces any "splash back" from heavy rain, which can soil the leaves of the tiny plants.

10. When completed, remove any loose soil from the rocks. If planted in the spring, the rock outcrop will soon mature, looking well-established by the end of its first summer.

ROCK PAVEMENT

*I*n some cases, rock outcrops that appear at ground level, creating an interesting pattern, are flat enough to walk over. This variation of a scree bed has been designed to appear like one of these outcrops, is one of the best ways of

displaying alpine plants, and makes an interesting feature that could be incorporated into most garden designs. One approach is to regard the area as a dry riverbed with stepping stones across it.

The Plants

Mat- and rosette-forming saxifrages and an antennaria provide pink, white, red, and yellow flowers in spring and summer. Dwarf blue and white columbines combine with pink dianthus, erodium, cranesbills, primrose-yellow rockroses, lilac phlox, and purple and white pasqueflowers. The silvery blue foliage of blue fescue grass and the black grass-like *Ophiopogon*, with the thistle-like foliage and pink and white flower spikes of morina, provide a contrast in shape and color.

(2) GRAHAM A PAVEY
Geranium cinereum "Ballerina"

(3)
Festuca glauca (Blue fescue)

(4)
Dianthus "Fusilier"

(6)
Pulsatilla vulgaris alba (Pasqueflower)

(10)
Saxifraga "Peter Pan"

(11)
Erodium reichardii

(16) *Pulsatilla vulgaris* (Pasqueflower)

(1) 2 *Ophiopogon planiscapus* "Nigrescens"

(5) *Saxifraga* x *edithiae* "Bridget"

(7) *Antennaria microphylla*

(8) *Phlox subulata* "Emerald Cushion Blue"

(9) *Aquilegia alpina* (Alpine columbine)

(12) *Saxifraga* "Schwefelblute" (Flowers of sulphur)

(13) *Morina longifolia*

(14) *Saxifraga moschata* "Cloth of Gold"

(15) 2 *Helianthemum* "Wisley Primrose"

Planting Plan

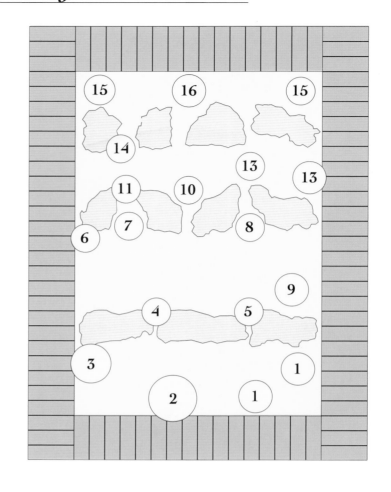

Flowering Season

Early spring to early summer.

Materials

Alpine planting mix (see page 147) •
90 bricks • Bricklayer's line •
Bricklayer's trowel • Lean mix (see
(see page 145) • Brick hammer • Mulching
mat • Selected rockery stone • Spade •
Level • Garden trowel

CARE
The occasional neatening to remove any dead foliage or flower heads is all that should be needed.

1. First mark out the pattern, then dig
out a trench about 9 inches wide and
6 inches deep. Line the excavation with
2 inches of lean mix.

2. Lay bricks in the pattern shown,
using a level to keep them straight and
a bricklayer's line to maintain a straight
line. Prepare the soil in the base of the
excavation by spreading a 2 inch layer
of sharp sand across the surface and
incorporating it into the top spade's
depth of soil.

3. To keep weeds down, lay the
mulching mat across the surface and
cover with a 4 inch layer of alpine
planting mix. Place selected stones in
the pattern desired. Here, we are
simulating strata rising to the surface
and have been careful to follow the
contours in the stone.

4. Lay the plants out in their position for planting.

5. Some plants will look at their best if growing in cracks between the stones. Remove the plant from its pot and squeeze the rootball to a shape where it will fit easily into the allocated space.

6. Before planting, tease out the roots from the rootball to make sure that the plant grows away well. Cut a cross in the mulching mat and plant through it.

7. Spread a layer of pea-size pebbles or fine gravel across the surface, being careful to cover the soil completely.

8. Lift any spreading plants, and gently push the stones underneath.

9. The pebbles look good and will keep the soil cool around the roots, something which many alpines appreciate. They also protect the small leaves from "splash back" in heavy rainstorms, an action which soils them and can cause some damage.

10. A mature scree bed makes an attractive garden feature. It is the perfect way to grow alpines.

BILL SHAW

BILL SHAW

BUBBLE FOUNTAIN

*F*lowing water, perhaps cascading over a rock, pouring from an overturned urn, or simply bubbling over stones will enhance any garden. This project shows how to make a basic bubble fountain, the perfect addition to any scree bed or small rock garden.

As a variation, a hole could be drilled through the center of a large rock, and the fountain pipe extended through it so water bubbles up through the hole and cascades down the sides of the rock. This could be incorporated into any kind of rock garden to give the appearance of an emerging spring.

Materials

Cobblestones • Selected stones •
2 engineering bricks • 1 extension pipe
• 2 galvanized wire frames,
30 inches square • Hose
• Spade or shovel • Level
• Submersible water pump,
216 gallons per hour
• Water tank, 20 inches deep by
26 inches diameter

CARE

Treat the water with an algicide to make sure algae does not collect on the stones.

The Plants

The big round leaves of heartleaf bergenia, tall variegated iris, glaucous gray parahebe with its dainty blue flowers, a waving grass, and a spreading, yellow-foliaged, dwarf yew provide all-year-round contrast and color around the bubbling water.

Iris foetidissima "Variegata"

Parahebe catarractae

Bergenia cordifolia "Purpurea"

Taxus baccata "Repens Aurea"

Pennisetum alopecuroides

Planting Plan

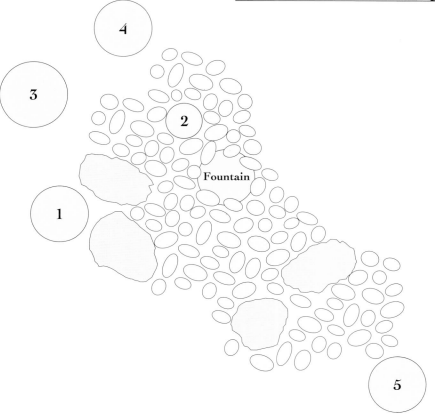

1. Dig a hole large enough for the water tank.

2. The hole should be a little larger than the tank to allow room to work.

3. Using a level, make sure the tank is straight. Adjust by adding or removing soil from the base of the excavation. When positioned correctly, fill with water, still using the level to make sure the tank remains straight.

4. To make sure that the water pump is at the right level, place two engineering bricks in the base of the tank.

5. Place the water pump on the bricks. Make sure the extension pipe extends above the water level.

6. Place one of the wire frames across the tank, insuring the extension pipe protrudes in the center.

7. To make sure the smaller cobblestones do not fall through the mesh, place the second wire frame at right angles to the first. Place the cobblestones loosely over the frame.

8. The water pump will require power. This is best supplied through a plastic conduit from the house.

9. Adjust the flow of water using a combination of the faucet on the pump and cobblestones piled around the end of the pipe. Be patient, it can take some time to get the flow just right.

10. Add selected large, round cobblestones for effect. These are sometimes referred to as "ostrich eggs."

11. Push pea-size pebbles up around the cobblestones to integrate the bubble fountain with the surrounding scree bed.

12. Grassy and spiky leaves are a good choice to accompany a bubble fountain and cobblestones. Here, we have planted *Iris foetidissima* "Variegata."

13. Low-growing alpines look good cascading over cobblestones.

14. Bubble fountains are perfect as an addition to a scree bed.

15. Bubble fountains are a versatile garden feature, and can even be incorporated into a small bed close to a patio area.

GRAHAM A PAVEY

RYL. NOWELL'S GARDEN . RHS CHELSEA FLOWER SHOW

16. When the basic fountain has been installed, there are an infinite number of variations for the fountain, from drilled boulders to various containers of all shapes and sizes.

STONE SINK GARDEN

*B*efore porcelain came into common use, natural stone was carved to create sinks, and these old, worn stone containers, so treasured by

gardeners, are the perfect choice for period and country gardens. They can look good on each side of a farmhouse doorway.

Materials

A stone sink,
24 inches x 16 inches x 6 inches
• Garden trowel • Pebbles
• Alpine planting mix (see page 147)
• Small piece of rock • Stone chips

CARE

Remove any dead leaves or flower heads, as necessary.

Flowering Season

Early to late spring.

The Plants

Evergreen mats of foliage are provided by an androsace, a rock pink, phlox, saxifrages, and red houseleeks, while a dwarf juniper provides an upright feature. The delightful pink flowers of the androsace, dwarf pinks, phlox, and saxifrage, the blue of *Anemone blanda,* and a yellow saxifrage glow throughout the spring.

5

Saxifraga "Silver Cushion"

6

Sempervivum "Black Prince" (Houseleek)

1

Juniperus communis "Compressa"

7

Phlox subulata "Temiskaming"

3

Saxifraga x *elisabethae* "Primrose Dame"

8

Anemone blanda

2 *Dianthus* "Pike's Pink"

4 *Androsace sempervivoides*

Planting Plan

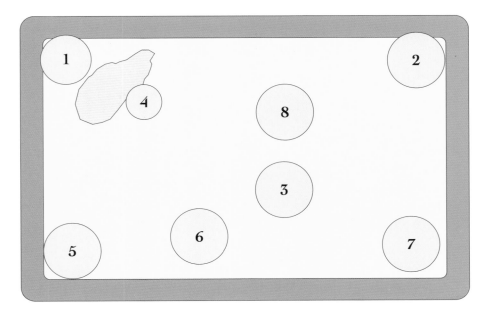

1. Old stone troughs are often already covered with patinas of lichen and moss, all of which add to their attraction.

2. Place some crockery shards over the drainage hole, and line the base of the sink with a layer of pebbles. Room is limited, so this cannot be too deep. Fill with alpine planting mixture up to the rim, and consolidate well.

3. Place a small piece of rock close to one corner for effect. This could be anything, but tufa would be a good choice.

4. Remove each plant from its pot by inverting it and gently squeezing the sides. Tease out the roots from the rootball before planting.

5. After planting, spread a layer of stone chips around the plants. Make sure that all areas are covered, lifting any spreading plants to push the stone chips underneath.

6. The plants in the final planted-up container will soon be well-established.

SINK GARDEN

*G*enuine stone sinks are popular containers for alpines, but are hard to find. However, this old glazed porcelain sink can be converted to make an effective and charming alternative.

Flowering Season

Spring

Materials

Alpine planting mix (see page 147)
• An old glazed sink, about 11 inches x 24 inches wide x 18 inches side width
• Bricklayer's trowel
• Crockery shards • Old paintbrush
• PVA-based adhesive or bonding agent • Sharp sand, cement, and sphagnum peatmoss, strained and lumps removed

The Plants

Bright pink thrift and alpine pinks mingle with brilliant blue trumpet-shaped gentians, unusual pink-and-white-flowered alpine phlox, white saxifrage and phlox, yellow sisyrinchium, and saxifrage. The silver, blue, and green evergreen foliage of the dwarf juniper, thrift, pinks, gentian, saxifrages, and grass-like sisyrinchium provide all-year-round charm.

(1)

Juniperus communis "Compressa"

(2)

Gentiana acaulis

(5)

Armeria maritima "Dusseldorfer Stolz"

(6)

Saxifraga x *elisabethae* "Primrose Dame"

(7) *Phlox subulata* "Kimono"

(3) *Sisyrinchium californicum*

(4) *Saxifraga* "Whitehills"

(8) *Dianthus* "La Bourboule"

(9) *Phlox subulata* "Maischnee"

167

Planting Plan

1. Clean the sink thoroughly and leave it to dry. Score the surface with a glass cutter, file, or tile cutter to make a good contact for the adhesive and hypertufa mixture.

2. Give the sink two coats of adhesive, leaving both to completely dry before progressing. A third and final coat should be brushed on immediately before step 3.

CARE

The gentian needs an acid soil, so make sure only rainwater is used when watering.

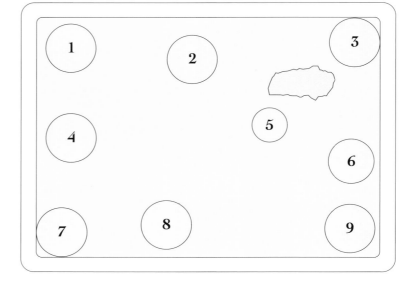

3. Mix enough hypertufa to cover the sink, using 1 part sand, 1 part cement, and 2 parts peatmoss. Mix the sand and cement thoroughly, and then add the peatmoss, which should be moistened first. Mix thoroughly and add a little water at a time, until the mixture is sufficiently moist to adhere to the sides of the sink.

4. Spread a fairly thin layer of hypertufa onto the sink (approximately 1 inch), and make sure this covers over the top edge and down inside the container. Before the mixture dries, square off the rim to simulate a smooth stone edge.

5. When the initial hardening has occurred, allow the trough to dry slowly by covering with plastic or damp burlap for a day or two. Line the base of the sink with a generous layer of crockery shards for drainage.

6. Position the plants for planting. Care should be taken in selecting plants suitable for a sink garden to make sure that they are not going to outgrow the space available.

7. Prepare each plant for planting by teasing the roots from the rootball.

9. Place the finished container in its final position, supported on bricks to aid drainage even more. The project will soon develop if planted in the spring, and will be well-established by the end of the first summer.

8. After planting, spread a layer of stone chips or horticultural gravel over the whole surface of the container. Lift the edge of any trailing plants and push the gravel underneath. This mulch will help to protect the plants and create a friendly environment for them.

10. Set aside an area in the garden devoted to these stone sinks. A graveled area as part of a patio is the perfect place, where an odd number, perhaps three or five, can be set out in a group.

TUFA GARDEN

Tufa is a very light material used to create walls in conservatories and ferneries, and on the inside walls of courtyards and cloister gardens.

Large chunks of tufa embedded into a scree bed and planted with various alpines make an unusual garden feature that always attracts attention.

Flowering Season

There are odd splashes of color through the year, but the main flowering season will be late spring through to mid-summer.

Materials

Alpine planting mix (see page 147)
• 2 pieces of tufa • Electric drill
• Large-diameter drill bit • Teaspoon

CARE
Virtually none. Keep well watered in dry weather.

The Plants

The silver, green, and purple sedum grows low, and tumbles over rocks and ground wherever it is planted, and the tiny alpine erinus will happily seed itself around, popping up in the tiniest cracks between rocks to show its bright pink flowers. In contrast, the houseleek, with its tiny white hairs, gives the impression it is covered with a spider's web. An androsace, rock pinks, and a saxifrage provide colorful pink and yellow flowers.

2 Androsace sarmentosa

Sedum spathulifolium "Cape Blanco"

Saxifraga x apiculata

Sempervivum arachnoideum

2 Dianthus "Pink Jewel"

Erinus alpinus "Dr Hahnle"

Planting Plan

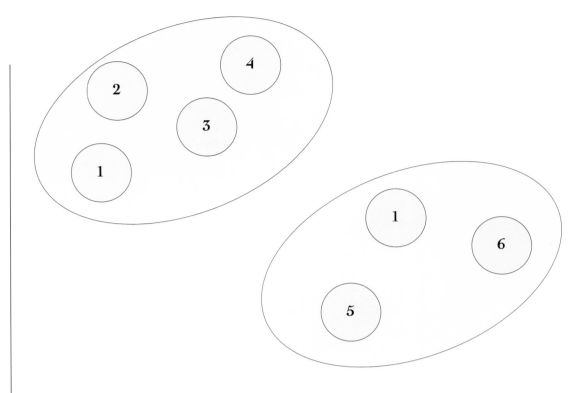

1. Before making any holes, decide where your plants would look best. The patina in the stone can be attractive, and you may want to leave it exposed.

2. An extra pair of hands will be needed for this step. After you have decided where the holes are to be drilled, hold the stone firmly, using the extra pair of hands.

3. Drill a hole sufficiently large enough to take the rootball of the plant to be used (this can be squashed down to fit, so do not make the hole too large). The hole can be made with an old screwdriver, but this is more time-consuming.

4. Remove the tufa dust with the teaspoon. The dust is useful and should be incorporated into the alpine planting mix.

5. Backfill the hole with alpine planting mix. Not all alpines are suitable for growing in tufa, so consult a reliable alpine nursery for advice.

6. Remove the plant from its pot by inverting it and gently squeezing the sides. Squash the rootball to make sure it fits comfortably into the hole; if necessary, remove some of the soil – do not be afraid, the plants are quite tough.

7. The plant must be consolidated. Do this by firming with the handle end of the teaspoon, adding more alpine planting mix, as necessary. When planted, a gentle tug should not dislodge it. The roots of the alpine will invade the tufa itself in time, and will live quite happily in a soil-free environment.

8. After the tufa is planted up, one-third of it should be buried in the ground (or soft sand). The capillary action of the tufa will then draw water and nutrients from the ground below.

ALPINES IN PAVING

A good way of deciding where to grow a plant in a garden is to look at how it grows in its native environment. Alpines like to grow in holes in rocks and among loose stones, and these would be perfect choices for softening a paved area, particularly a patio.

One of the rules of garden design states that the size of the patio should be equal to one-third the height of the house to the eaves. In some cases the paved area can often look too large and unwelcoming, so growing plants between the cracks in the paving helps soften the area.

The Plants

Here, delightfully colored and often aromatic foliage is used to create a patchwork of evergreen underfoot. From its solid mat of ground-covering, steel-blue foliage, New Zealand burr produces fuzzy, round reddish-brown flowers, and the little alpine alchemilla has the crinkled foliage and lime green flowers of its larger cousin – lady's mantle. The aromatic chamomile, used to create chamomile lawns, the Corsican mint, and two thymes – one with green-and-gold leaves – all have aromatic leaves, especially when crushed. The evergreen phlox provides a splash of color with its crimson flowers in late spring and early summer.

1 *2 Acaena* "Blue Haze" (New Zealand burr)

2 *Thymus* "Doone Valley"

3 *Chamaemelum nobile* "Treneague"

4 *Phlox douglasii* "Red Admiral"

5 *Thymus herba-barona* (Caraway thyme)

6 *Alchemilla alpina*

7 *Mentha requienii* (Corsican mint)

CARE
An occasional trim of the plants will keep them compact.

173

Planting Plan

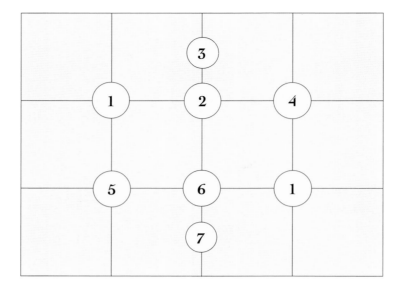

Flowering Season

The plants in this scheme have been chosen primarily for their attractive ground-covering foliage, but the main flourish is in late spring to midsummer.

Materials

Alpine planting mix (see page 147)
• Bricklayer's trowel • Chisel
• Rubble • Lean mix (see page 145)
• Brick hammer • Gloves • Spade
• Level

1. Mark out the area, and dig out the soil to a depth suitable for accepting the layer of rubble and lean mix.

2. Break off the corners of the paving slabs where plants are to be planted. Mark the piece of slab to be removed by gently tapping the chisel with the brick hammer all the way around the piece.

3. Give the corner one sharp tap with the brick hammer, and it should break off. If it does not, then repeat step 2. If the corner does not come away cleanly, it will not matter, because the plants will cover any mistakes.

4. Line the base of the excavation with rubble, and backfill with a lean mix of sand and cement. Lay the paving stones using a level and the brick hammer handle to make sure the whole paved area is straight and firm.

5. Brush alpine planting mix into the spaces and cracks left in the paving.

6. Lay the plants out where they are to be planted. The plants chosen here are all ground-hugging, many of which are aromatic when stepped on.

7. Remove each plant from its container and reshape the rootball before planting into its position. Use the alpine planting mix to consolidate each plant.

8. After planting, the plants will soon begin to cover the paving slabs. In time, the paving will change dramatically, covered with a mat of many different colors.

ACKNOWLEDGMENTS

I would like to give special thanks to my wife, Chris; Sandra
and Richard Oliver, Angela Whiting, Barry Johnson and all
the staff at Anglia Alpines and Herbs Ltd; David, Jason and
Paul of DJ Landscapes; Maureen Cattlin, Ian, Mike, Ray,
Mags and all the staff at Milton Ernest Garden Centre and
Waterways Pet and Aquatic Centre; Ian and
Susie Pasley-Tyler of Coton Manor; Stonemarkets Ltd;
Steve Woods and the staff at Tacchi's Garden Scene; and to
Chas Bolton at Wright's Builders Merchants.

Picture Credits
The Publisher would like to thank the following for
providing photographs and for permission to reproduce
copyright material:

Graham A. Pavey; Garden Matters; Harry Smith Collection;
Bill Shaw, Floracolour; Richard Key; Heather Angel;
Diana Grenfell; and R. Harkness & Co.

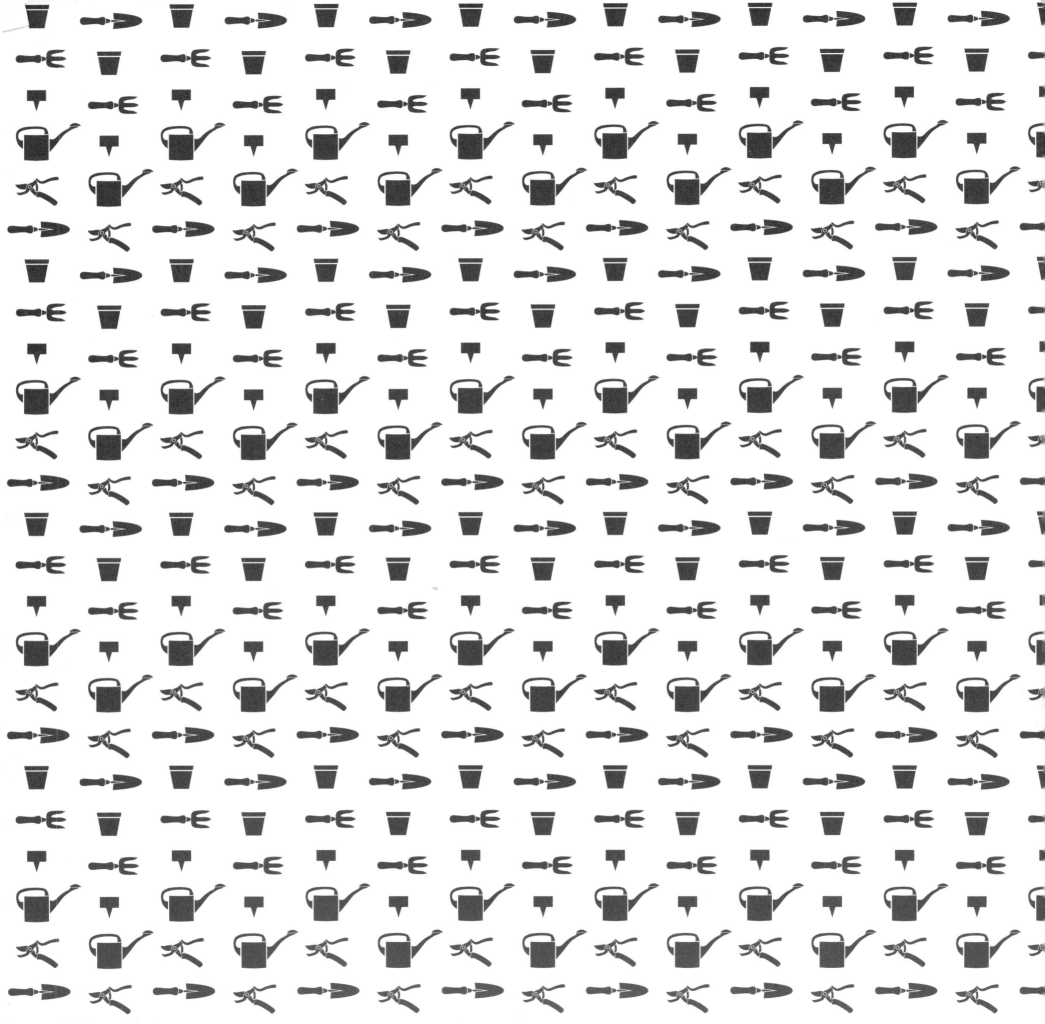